Scrap Quilts

For Material Girls

by

Brenda Henning

Bear Paw Productions
4015 Iona Circle
Anchorage, AK 99507

Dedication

To the quilt groups I belong to: the Material Girls and the Sourdough Stitchers.
We are as different as patches in a quilt. Of course that quilt is a crazy quilt.

Acknowledgments

Thank you to Kathryn Rhea and Debbie Repasky for sharing their quilts with us all.

Thanks to Benartex for donation of the Barn Dance fabric used in **Road to Oklahoma** and **Autograph Lattice**.

Many thanks to Hobbs Bonded Fibers for providing the Heirloom Cotton Batting used in all of the quilts.

And my biggest thank you goes to my husband, Richard, and three children, Beth, Christi and Joshua. Thank you for putting up with a quilting Mom — missed meals, fast food and unwashed laundry!

Credits

Written and illustrated by Brenda Henning.
Photography by Mark Frey of Seattle, WA, and Ken Wagner of Seattle, WA.
Edited by Marcia Harmening.
Machine quilting by Norma Kindred and Brenda Harris.
Printed in the United States of America.

ISBN 0-9648878-2-7

Scrap Quilts for Material Girls©
© 1997 by Brenda Henning
Bear Paw Productions
4015 Iona Circle
Anchorage, AK 99507
(907) 349-7873

Contents

Introduction

As a small child I remember a quilt that was my "security" blanket. No one else in my family can remember that quilt or who made it for me. As a preteen, I taught myself to sew on a treadle sewing machine. Using discarded fabrics, I sewed doll clothes and other small childish items.

Piecing quilt tops was a natural extension of my sewing skills. Unfortunately, I had no one to tell me how I could possibly make the four inch squares all the same size. My early quilts were well-loved and worn. No one seemed to care that the seams did not line up or that they were tied and not quilted with tiny stitches.

Scrap quilts have always held a special place in my heart. All of my early quilts were made from leftover clothing construction scraps, or pirated from the pile of discarded or outgrown clothing left by my siblings. Those quilts still evoke memories of the clothing, events attended in the clothing, or the person the clothing had once belonged.

Quilting is best when shared with friends. I am a member of two groups. Each group meets monthly. We make blocks for each member in turn. The Material Girls are pictured below. The Sourdough Stitchers are not pictured. Those members include: Donna George, Lela Walicki, Debbie Repasky, Mary Walicki Sailor, and Pat Syta.

The Material Girls gather monthly to exchange blocks, taking a break during the summer months to allow us to enjoy the short Alaskan summer. Photographed from left: Brenda Faust, Brenda Harris, Jan Fithian (hiding), Joyce Baker, Joyce Dale, Sharon Upchurch, Marcia Brown, Von Brown, Marie Lee, Nancy Prince, Dawn Cross, Brenda Henning (hiding), Cheri Cooper, Joanne Lawrence, and Joyelene Hendrickson. Not pictured is Cher Chu. Cher is a member that moved out of stated but chose to continue making blocks with the group.

Chapter 1 Collecting Fabric

Scrap quilts of yesteryear were created out of necessity. Fabric scraps were not to be wasted. Quilts could be pieced using scraps of fabric too small to be put to other use. While frugality may have determined what fabric was used in quilt piecing, the great creative energies of the pioneer women can be seen in the antique quilts still with us today. Care was taken to cut patches of uniform size and shape. If the scrap was too small to be cut into the patch necessary, two smaller pieces might be sewn together to form that patch. Great accuracy was accomplished even with the crude tools available to the quilters.

Lessons Learned

Twenty years ago when I started piecing, the fabrics in my quilts were an array of leftovers from my clothing construction projects. Cotton, cotton/polyester blends, wool blends, denim, and corduroy were all combined into quilt tops. I have learned many lessons from those early forays into quilting.

1) I am a dismal failure when it comes to using cardboard templates. Thank goodness for template plastic and rotary cutting tools. Without these newfangled inventions I would still be struggling with cardboard templates and scissors.

2) I used many fabrics together. I won't even admit some of the strange combinations that I tried. What these combinations taught me is that it is best to use like fabrics and fibers together. Corduroy, denim, and polyester blends are much stronger than 100% cotton quilting fabric. While this may not be readily apparent, over the life of a quilt the strength of the polyester fabric will weaken the adjacent cotton patches, possibly resulting in tears to the cotton patch.

3) For the same reason I use 100% cotton thread with cotton fabric. This is a lesson I learned the hard way. My early quilts were stitched using the cotton wrapped polyester thread that my mother had in the sewing cabinet. After use and washing, the polyester core thread

literally **cut** the cotton fabrics at the seam line.

Remember, these quilts were a mixture of fibers and fabric weights. I am sure that this mix added to the stress along the seams. Unfortunately, the patches are ruined, and would need to be replaced to restore the quilts. My lesson has been learned. My quilts are now sewn with only 100% cotton thread, 50 wt./ 3 ply. If the thread should weaken and break, the seam can be restitched. It is much more difficult to replace damaged fabric patches.

The last quilt of my early era graces the dog's kennel. I cannot bring myself to repair that atrocity, but I also cannot bear to throw it away!

4) As a self-taught teen-age quilter, I was interested in having a completed quilt. I had no hand quilting skill, nor did I have anyone to teach me the skill. My quilts were tied using acrylic yarn that was on hand.

When quilts are tied or scantily quilted, the fabric is allowed greater freedom and causes additional wear to the patches. A quilt that has been heavily quilted by hand or machine, will be more stable and have a much longer life. Heavy quilting will also reduce the strain on individual patches and seams caused by mixed fabric selections and polyester sewing thread.

Fiber Content

When collecting fabric today, I gather only 100% cottons to be used in my quilts. Cotton will take a crease when the seams are pressed and forgive the quilter when it is necessary to ease a seam to fit. Cotton can be pressed at high temperatures and resist scorching.

My days of clothing construction are past and I no longer have polyester, denim or corduroy scraps. A move three years ago gave me an excellent reason to donate all of those fabric pieces to the local clothing room.

If you have an existing fabric stash that you would like to use, you may want to determine the fiber content of the pieces before you begin. If I am uncertain of a fabric's origin, I burn a small scrap of the fabric in question. If the fabric burns away to ash, the fiber is most likely natural in origin. If the fabric seems to melt and leave small "beads" when burned, it is most likely a synthetic.

Scrap Sources
Fabric pieces used in my scrap quilts are from a number of sources. I do maintain a scrap basket. The pieces languishing there are generally small scraps, odd triangles, bits of leftover strips, etc. Quite frankly, I am often unwilling to dig into the basket in search of the "right" piece of fabric.

Most often my scrap quilts are selections of fabric pulled from my stash. Terrific basic colors, backgrounds, border fabrics, and backing are purchased in large quantities (sometimes by the bolt). Fabrics that do not fit into the above four categories are purchased one yard at a time. It is rare that I will purchase fabric in lengths shorter than one yard.

As I use the one-yard pieces, one raw edge is cut clean. This end is used for all strip cutting. The opposite raw edge is used when I need to cut individual squares or just a few pieces that do not require a complete strip.

When strips are cut and not used up the remainder of the strip is tucked back into the folded yardage. By treating "scraps" in this manner, pieces are not mashed and wrinkled in the bottom of a scrap basket, never to be seen again. When that yardage is unfolded, that cut strip may be exactly what is required for the current project.

Another "source" for the numerous pieces required for scrap quilts might be one of the terrific fabric collections being produced by the fabric manufacturers. Two such quilts may be found in this book, *Road To Oklahoma,* on page 45, and *Autograph Lattice*, on page 49. Both quilts were created using the *Barn Dance* collection of fabrics from *Benartex.*

In some cases, the fabric collections have been designed and colored to work as a unit. If the collection is large enough, you may be able to achieve a "scrap" look without departing from the collection. This is a great way to develop a scrap look without the mental anguish some quilters feel when selecting numerous fabrics

Chapter 2   Selecting Fabric

Fabric selection has long been one of the most painful tasks for my students. I am here to tell you that this skill can be learned! I am living proof!

I started quilting 20+ years ago. I did not become a compulsive quilter until fourteen years ago. At that time I started purchasing fabrics to make a nine fabric quilt. What an experience. The shop was NO help and the quilt was never finished. I truly believed that I would never quilt again.

My next experience was a four-fabric Christmas quilt. The selection process was easy because even I understood that all I really needed was a light background, a solid red, a solid green, and a red and green print.

The third quilt was an Amish basket. This too was no real difficulty. I did break the rules about true Amish color selection, but I didn't learn this until my quilt book collection enlarged to include such a book. This quilt was a "real" quilt. I hand quilted it myself. It turned out pretty well, all things considered.

By the time I was ready to undertake the fourth quilt, I knew that I needed to ask someone to help with the colors. I departed from my "comfort zone" with the colors chosen, and the quilt was terrific. To make a long story short, I found employment at this shop. I spent many enjoyable days and evenings helping customers select fabrics for their many quilts. The early days were more difficult. I learned as much from the customers about fabric as they might have learned from me. (Truth be told, I think I learned more!)

Many of my students have commented on my ability to use color. This is not a genetic gift. The ability to use color is a learned skill. I have had no formal art training beyond junior high art and drafting.

The fear felt by many color-timid quilters may stem from the lack of basic color wheel knowledge. I do not believe that one needs a detailed education about color theory, just a few highlights. I would encourage anyone that does

not already own a color wheel to purchase a good artist's color wheel at your local art supply store.

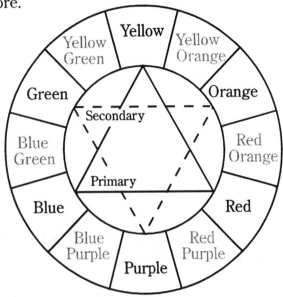

Color Wheel
The color wheel diagramed above shows the basic color relationships as you travel around the wheel. The **primary colors** are yellow, red, and blue. They are the base colors that are mixed to derive all other colors. The **secondary colors** are orange, green, and purple. Secondary colors result from the mixture of two primary colors: red + yellow = orange, etc. **Tertiary colors** result from the mixing of a primary and a secondary color: blue + purple = blue-purple.

Color Schemes
The basic color schemes outlined below are but a few of the ways colors can be used together harmoniously. Please remember that a quilt is your personal creation. If the color scheme is harmonious in your eyes, do not listen to anyone who would tell you otherwise. Color selection and use are very personal decisions.

1) A Monochromatic Color Scheme incorporates fabrics of one color family. The *Friendship Star* quilt on page #44 is a monochromatic quilt. Many shades of green have been combined to create this remarkable quilt. The monochromatic scheme is the simplest of all color combinations because only one color family is involved. The design is created through change in color value.

2) An Analogous Color Scheme incorporates three color families that are adjacent to one another on the color wheel. Because analogous colors are closely related, the colors flow gracefully and are comfortable together. Examples might be: a) yellow, yellow-orange, and orange as seen in a sunset; b) blue, blue-green, and green that you might see together at the lake; c) red, red-orange, and orange of the fall leaf display.

An even broader application of analogous colors are when three more general color families are used: green, blue, and purple; or red, orange, and yellow.

The *Tablescraps* and *Kaleidoscope* quilts pictured on pages 43 and 52 are both examples of an extended analogous color scheme. Why use three color families when more is better!

3) A Complementary Color Scheme uses two colors directly opposite one another on the color wheel. Each color has only one complement: a) red and green, no wonder Christmas quilts are so dynamic; b) purple and yellow, I've always loved pansies; and c) blue and orange.

These three basic color schemes are just the beginning of color use. Use them as color guidelines or disregard them entirely. Your quilt ought to reflect you and your color sense.

Selecting a Color Palette
Before you begin to sort through your fabric stash, think for a moment about what you would like your completed quilt to look like.

1) Choose one or two colors to base the color selection process. These may be your favorite

colors or colors that fit your decor.

2) Select fabrics from your collection that fit the chosen color scheme. Interpret the color broadly. If you are working with green, consider the blue-greens and the yellow-greens, as well as the true greens.

If you are working with two or more colors, repeat the selection process for each color chosen.

3) You may wish to build a "bridge" between the base fabrics. A range of blues may be used to fill the gap between green and purple. By bridging a gap, you be creating an analogous color scheme. Study the color use in *Tablescraps* and *Kaleidoscope* for example.

4) As you are building your fabric grouping, step back and inspect your fabric from afar. Viewing the fabric from a distance can reveal gaps in your color gradation. Sometimes it is not possible to view the fabric from across a large room. If this is the case, consider viewing the fabric through: **a)** a camera view finder; **b)** a door peephole, available at your local hardware store; **c)** the wrong end of binoculars; or **d)** a reducing glass.

5) Have you forgotten any fabrics in your quest for the perfect grouping? Many fabrics will be represented in a scrap quilt, and each one will appear only a few times. "Uglies" can actually be the spark that excites a calm grouping while some large prints cut up nicely into small pieces to add movement.

6) It is best to add many fabrics to the grouping during the gathering process. Pieces that do not quite fit can be removed later as your vision solidifies.

Establishing Control
can be a challenge when working with a scrap quilt. Be firm and take one of the following suggestions if control is a problem.

1) Limit fabrics to your chosen color scheme. Haphazard color selections across the color wheel without any unifying element, can cause a chaotic looking quilt with no place for your eye to rest.

2) Neutrals can be used to establish order in an otherwise busy collection. A calming neutral background has been used in a number of the quilts photographed in this book. An array of similar tan fabrics was used in *Broken Windmill*, page 42, to create the controlling background.

3) A consistent sashing can be used to frame and subdue the developing pattern. *Autograph Lattice* uses a diagonal strip in each block to create a pseudo-sashing look which helps to create an order.

4) Careful color placement can be used to create uniformity and a pleasing secondary pattern as shown in *Road to Oklahoma*, *Autograph Lattice*, and *Broken Windmill*. If allowed to fall in an uncoordinated fashion, the dark values and colors would create a noisy disorder.

Determining Value

Value can be defined as the lightness or darkness of a color. To this point, most of your attention has been focused on selection of colors to fulfill the color scheme. To construct some of the quilts photographed in this text, you will need to separate the fabrics by value.

The pattern that develops in the *Pioneer Braid*, page 41, is due entirely to the placement of light and dark values.

Study the fabrics used in the *Tablescraps* blocks. High contrast between the dark and light color values creates a very distinctive secondary pattern. Low contrast values allow the pattern to disappear into the myriad of fabrics used.

"Value" is relative. It is a term used to compare a fabric's lightness or darkness to the surrounding fabrics.

Arrange your fabrics from light to dark, regardless of color.

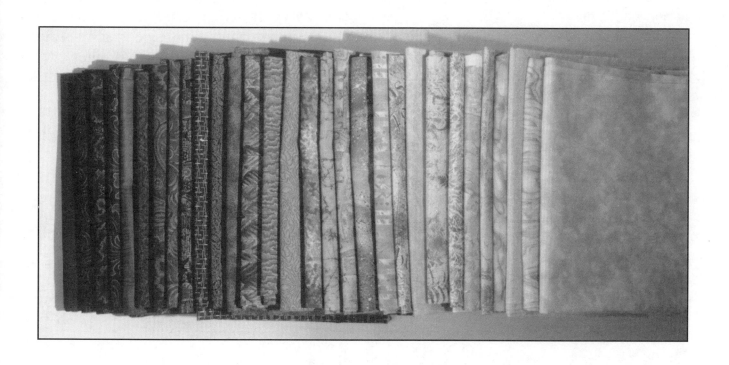

Chapter 3 Cutting Fabric

Rotary Cutting Tools

The **rotary cutter** is a razor knife that resembles a pizza cutter. The blade is very sharp and deserves to be treated with utmost respect. This amazing tool has revolutionized quilt making, nearly replacing scissors. I recommend a rotary cutter that has a manual safety guard. Some rotary cutters available on the market have a spring-loaded guard that can accidentally retract when dropped, exposing the razor sharp blade and cutting your hand or foot. The spring-loaded guards protect you from only the most minor of blade "bumps." The rotary cutters that have a manually closing safety guard, such as Olfa® and Fiskar®, require that you consciously close the guard after every cut. Learn to make a habit of closing the guard every time!! An exposed blade on the work surface can lead to tragic results, accidentally cut fabric or worse — cut fingers and bloodstained fabric. **Do not** leave a rotary cutter unattended around a curious toddler or young child.

I prefer to use the **Olfa®** rotary cutter. This particular rotary cutter can be used both right and left-handed.

To ensure the life of the blade, the rotary cutter must be used only on a compatible cutting surface. The self-healing **cutting mats** are a necessary tool. While the mats come in many sizes, purchase the largest cutting mat that you can afford. The 24" x 36" cutting mat is worth every dime.

Omnigrid® is my ruler of preference. The Omnigrid® brand is the most accurate of all rulers that I have worked with. It is very important that all of your rulers are accurate and agree with each other. Compare the markings of all rulers in your collection. If any ruler does not measure up, discard it!! The markings on your rotary mat must also agree with the rulers you have chosen to use.

Squaring Up Yardage

• Fold your fabric in half lengthwise, wrong sides together, selvage edges even. You may need to shift one selvage to the right or left to eliminate wrinkles along the folded edge. Once this has been accomplished, fold the fabric again, lengthwise, bringing the folded edge even with the selvage edges. The fabric will now be folded into four thicknesses, and measure about 10 1/2" wide. Fabric folded to this width can be cut into strips without repositioning your ruler hand.

• Lay the folded fabric horizontally on your gridded cutting mat. The folded edge should be nearest you. Place the fold along a horizontal line of the mat. This will allow you to place your ruler along a vertical mat marking, guaranteeing a straight cut. If you are right-handed, the bulk of your fabric should be on the right, and you will start cutting from the left side. This will be reversed for a left-handed person.

• The rotary cutter is held with the blade perpendicular to the mat and against the edge of the ruler. If the blade is held at any other angle, the cutting will not be as effective and effortless. The rotary cutter is held in the palm of your hand with the index finger on the ridged surface of the handle. This placement helps you to better control the rotary cutter. You are in effect pointing it in the proper direction.

• Cut away from yourself using one smooth even stroke. **Do not** make short choppy cuts. This will give you a ragged edge. The first cut you make will be to trim off the ragged raw edge to square up the fabric. The clean edge will be perpendicular to the selvage. Trim sparingly to give the fabric a clean edge while wasting as little fabric as possible.

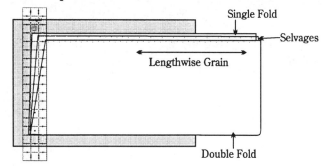

Cutting Strips

After the original cut has been made to square up the end of the yardage, you are ready to cut your first strip.

• Move the ruler to the right (left for a left-handed person) and align the squared off edge with the ruler marking for the strip width desired. Make sure that the correct marking lines up all along the cut edge, not just at one point!! **Measure twice and cut once!!**

• Cut along the right (left) side of the ruler. Be sure to keep your blade flush against the ruler, do not allow the ruler to shift. Lift the ruler and remove the strip without disturbing the yardage.

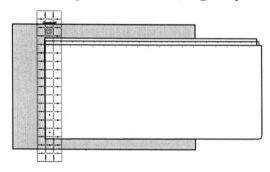

• Open the strip and look at it closely. The strip should be straight and of a consistent width. If your strip is not straight, refold your fabric and make certain that the edges are even. Also, make sure the original cut was made correctly, perpendicular to the folded edge.

• If it is necessary to cut a strip wider than your ruler, use the rulings of the cutting mat to measure the strip or square.

Subcutting Strips

• Squares and rectangles needed for piecing will be cut from strips. Cut the strip to the required width and open the double fold. You will be working with two layers of fabric and a single fold. If you are right handed, the selvages should be placed at the left. Trim off the first 1/2" to remove the selvages (more if needed) and square up the end of the strip. Use the mat markings to establish a perpendicular cut.

• Align the top edge of the ruler with the edge of the fabric, the bottom edge of the fabric should

line up with a ruler marking. Cut the squares or rectangles to the required dimension. Continue cutting from the strip to satisfy the number needed.

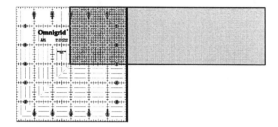

Half Square Triangles

Before I begin the triangle discussion, I feel that I must first apologize to the vast majority of quilters that have never cared for geometry and in all honesty have never seen a real need to learn the information presented. The triangle information that follows is very simplified. If you really care to know how the formula works, study the diagram to better understand. If you are like the majority, just accept the theory, why the information is necessary, and memorize the numbers.

Half square triangles are literally triangles that are one half of a square. The square is cut once from corner to corner, diagonally. This places the grain of the fabric along the two short sides of the right triangle.

A half square triangle is one of the most basic shapes used in quiltmaking. Therefore, it is very important to know when to use this type of triangle. Half square triangles are used whenever the short side of the triangle will fall at the edge of a quilt block or quilt top. This allows for the greatest stability and the least amount of stretch in these much handled positions.

When working with templates, as discussed on page 12, watch for the arrows that indicate grain (thread) lines. The location of these arrows will determine if the triangle is a half square triangle or a quarter square triangle (discussion to follow).

While there are many ways to create half square triangles, this text will focus on the most basic method. Half square triangles will begin as squares that are cut in half diagonally.

The formula below is **very** important for you to remember. It is the key to working with half square triangles!!

❧ Finished Size + 7/8" = Cut Square ❧

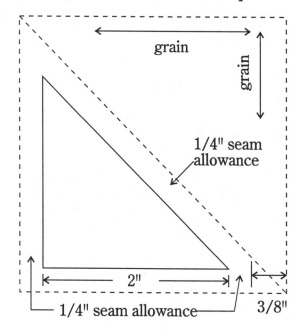

In the above diagram, 2" is the finished size of the triangle. As you can see, there is an additional 3/8" at the right that needs to be accounted for. Where does this 3/8" extension go when triangles are sewn together? These pieces are called "dog ears" and are trimmed from the completed unit. This eliminates bulk and prevents the shadow that a dog ear can create behind a light background fabric.

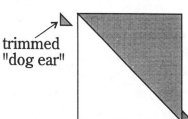

trimmed "dog ear"

Template Preparation and Use

Templates are necessary in the case of shapes that cannot be cut with a rotary cutter and standard rotary ruler. The pieces may be curved or involve angles that are not 30°, 60° or 45° angles.

Templates are generally made from frosted sheets of plastic that can be purchased at your local quilt shop. Template plastic is available with or without a 1/4" grid. The plastic can be easily cut with paper scissors, or a rotary cutter.

• Trace the template on to the plastic with a **sharp** pencil. I prefer to use a 0.5 mm mechanical lead pencil, it never dulls. It is helpful to use a small ruler to trace the straight lines.

• You may find that taping the plastic in place with drafting tape while tracing the template is necessary. Drafting tape removes easily from paper and will not harm your original pattern or book.

• Mark the grain line, if indicated, and all extra dots and lines that may be helpful as you construct the quilt block. It is a good idea to note block details on the template: such as the block name, block size, and template number or letter, if so titled.

• Very carefully, cut on the drawn line. Once the template is cut, place it on top of the original to make certain that the template has not "grown". It is very important that the template does not change size, shape, or angle.

Chapter 4 Machine Piecing

1/4" Seam Allowance

All of our seams will be sewn with a 1/4" seam allowance. It is of utmost importance to establish and maintain an accurate 1/4" seam allowance. Some of you will already have quilting experience and feel confident that you know where your 1/4" seam is. I would encourage you to do the following exercise anyway. Just humor me if nothing else. I have found that many of my students have misjudged their seam allowance and have been able to correct it with this exercise.

ર&ર&ર&ર&ર&

NOTE - You will actually be sewing with a **scant** 1/4" seam allowance. The difference will be taken up in the slight fold or "ridge" at the seam.

ર&ર&ર&ર&ર&

• To find your 1/4" seam allowance place a small ruler underneath your presser foot. When the needle is gently lowered, it should rest just to the right of the 1/4" mark on the right side of your ruler. If the needle were to pierce the ruler, the hole left by the needle would just graze the 1/4" marking on your ruler.

• With the presser foot holding the ruler in this position, carefully pivot the ruler so the markings on the left side of the ruler run parallel with the markings on the throat plate of your sewing machine.

• Once you are satisfied the ruler is positioned correctly, place a 1/2" x 3" strip of moleskin along the right edge of the ruler on the throat plate. Moleskin is a Dr. Scholl's® product, available at most groceries and pharmacies. The adhesive back of the moleskin will stick to the throat plate and give an edge to hold your seam allowance against. Moleskin gives more of an edge to follow than masking tape. It is not high enough that it will impede or pull out your pins.

1/4" Seam Test

• Cut 4 pieces of fabric 1 1/2" x 6". Sew these strips together along the lengthwise edge. Press the seams in one direction. After pressing, check that there are no "accordion" pleats at the seams. Press again if necessary.

• Measure your sewn unit, it should measure exactly 4 1/2" from raw edge to raw edge. The strips on either side should measure 1 1/4", and the center strips should each measure 1" wide.

• If your sewn unit doesn't measure exactly 4 1/2", you will need to adjust your moleskin. If the sewn unit is **wider** than 4 1/2", your seam allowance is too narrow and the moleskin should be moved to the right. If the sewn strip is **narrower** than 4 1/2", your seam allowance is too wide and the moleskin should be moved to the left.

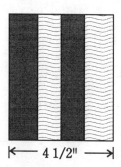

|← 4 1/2" →|

The amount that you need to move the moleskin is only one sixth of the amount that your strip differs from 4 1/2". Three seams are involved in the sewn strip, each seam involves two pieces of fabric — move the moleskin 1/6 of the difference.

It is a commonly held thought that the 1/4" **seam allowance** should be measured to check the accuracy of the stitching. Unfortunately, this does not work. The seam allowance is a scant 1/4". If anything is measured it ought to be the finished dimension of the fabric from the right side of the unit or quilt block.

I do not trust the 1/4" marking on my sewing machines. Usually the factory markings are accurate enough for clothing construction, but not for the precision demanded by quilting. I also do not recommend using the edge of your presser foot as a guide. Very few actually measure 1/4" from the needle.

If you have placed the moleskin exactly as described, and are still having problems stitching a 1/4" seam allowance, it may be your sewing machine that is being naughty. The feed dogs of some machines pull to the right, some to the left. Sewing machines are an eccentric lot! Adjust the moleskin to where the sewing machine demands that the edge of the fabric be held. This may not be at the mark 1/4" from the needle. Get to know your machine and work with its character flaws.

Strip Piecing

Not all piecing is accomplished by sewing individual squares and triangles together. Many units can be first sewn together in strip form and then, after the strips are subcut, the resulting units will be stitched together to form the intended square.
- The first step is to arrange the strips in the sequence that they will appear.
- Begin by sewing strips together in pairs.

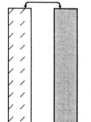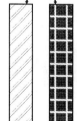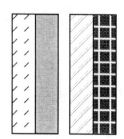

- After each pair is sewn, press the strips flat from the wrong side. This smooths any wrinkles caused by poor thread tension and sets the seam.

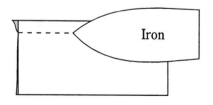

- Once you have set the seam, open the fabrics and press the seam from the right side. Pressing on the right side gives the visibility required to prevent accordion pleating at the seam. The seam allowances should be pressed in one direction for the greatest strength.

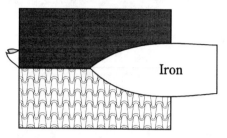

- Stitch strip pairs together and press.
- Once sewn and pressed, the strips may be subcut into the units necessary to complete the piecing of the block. Place the strip right side up on the cutting mat. Align a perpendicular marking of the ruler with a seam line and cut the strip to the width called for in the pattern.
- Reassemble the subcut units into the formation dictated by the pattern, stitch and press.

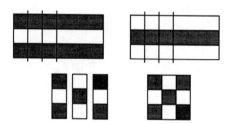

Chain Piecing

Chain piecing refers to the practice of stitching units one right after another without clipping the threads between the units.
- The first unit is stitched and left attached to the threads after passing under the presser foot.
- The second and following units are inserted under the presser foot one or two stitches after the previous unit has passed. No threads are cut.

This method saves thread and the time required to start each unit as an individual. It also allows you to repetitively piece the same unit and create a rhythm, thereby reducing mistakes.

Triangle Foundation Paper

Half square triangles are one of the most basic shapes used in quiltmaking. Unfortunately, they are also one of the most often distorted shapes. Gridded triangles have long been present in quilting instructions. Accuracy is greatly increased when half square triangles are pieced using gridded papers. Master triangle foundations may be found on pages 83 - 85. If you would prefer to use commercially prepared papers, refer to the sources listed on page 92, or check with your local quilt shop for availability.

1) Photocopy or trace the number of triangle papers necessary for your chosen quilt.

2) Cut the fabrics as indicated in the individual pattern. The rectangle or square cut will be slightly larger than the paper foundation.

3) Place two fabric pieces right sides together. Position a triangle paper on the wrong side of the light (background) fabric and pin the paper to the fabric pair

4) Starting at the dot, stitch on all dotted lines. Follow the numbered arrows for a continuous seam. Use a small stitch (15 - 20 stitches per inch), and a size 14 sewing machine needle, to better perforate the paper foundation.

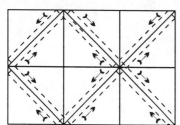

5) Cut on all solid lines using a rotary cutter and ruler. Each 6 1/4" pair will yield 8 half square triangle units. Each 6 1/4" x 9 1/8" pair will yield 12 half square triangle units.

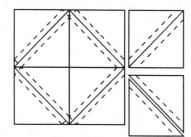

6) With the paper still attached, press the seam toward the dark fabric.

7) Remove the paper foundation. Place your thumb nail on the stitched seam at the center of the block. Pull the paper foundation from the square corner against your thumb nail. This will help to reduce the number of stitches lost at the seam ends.

8) Trim all dog ears.

Foundation Paper Piecing

Foundation piecing has been introduced because of the small pieces in the miniature bear paw blocks found in the Cabin Fever Bears quilt on page 53. This eliminates the need to cut tiny pieces and increases accuracy.

Points to Remember
• It is helpful to use a larger sewing machine needle, such as, a size 14 needle.
• Stitch with a shorter stitch length, 15 - 20 stitches per inch, to better perforate the paper.
• The lines on the pattern are the actual sewing lines. Sew directly on these lines.
• The fabric pieces will be placed on the **unmarked** side of the foundation paper, and the seam will be sewn from the marked side.
• The fabric pieces do not need to be cut precisely. After stitching, the excess will be trimmed to a 1/4" seam allowance. Take care to allow sufficient fabric to cover the area.
• The block is diagramed with the numerical sequence of fabric application.
• The foundation pattern will be the mirror image of the final product!!

Foundation Piecing Steps

1) Photocopy or trace the foundation piecing designs. If you choose to trace the designs, artist vellum works well.

2) Trim away the excess paper from the copied design, leaving 1/4" beyond the outermost line.

3) Cut a piece of background fabric for Section 1. The piece should be cut slightly larger than the area, allowing at least 1/4" for the seam allowance on all sides.

4) Place the fabric piece against the unmarked side of the foundation paper, position behind Section 1 and pin in place.

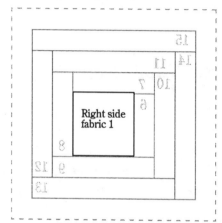

The back side of the foundation paper will be exposed and the right side of the fabric for section 1 will be showing. Pin in place or hold with a **small** dab of glue stick.

5) Cut a piece of fabric for Section 2. This piece should be slightly larger than the area, allowing at least 1/4" for the seam allowance on all sides. Position on top of Section 1 fabric, right sides together.

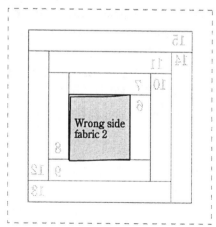

6) Flip the paper/fabric assembly over and with the marked side of the foundation facing up, stitch on the seam line between sections 1 and 2. Stitch past the end of the seam line on either end to anchor the fabric. There is no need to back-tack, the stitches are small and will not be pulled out.

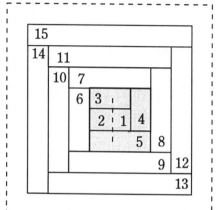

7) Finger press the seam to eliminate all pleats or carefully press the seam using an iron. This is a very important step. A poorly pressed seam may mean disaster later.

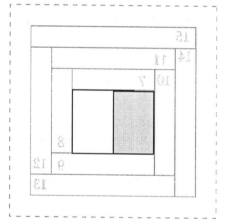

8) Continue adding pieces until all sections have been completely covered. Trim the edge of the block along the dotted line, leaving a 1/4" seam allowance.

9) After trimming, remove the foundation paper. Pinch the beginning of the seam between the thumb and forefinger of your "wrong" hand and gently pull away the paper, placing all excess force against the thumb nail holding the seam down. If removed in this manner, undue roughness will be reduced, stretching, and pulled stitches kept to a minimum.

Chapter 5   Quilt Patterns

This chapter contains complete patterns for twelve different quilts. All of the designs are multi-sized for your convenience. The patterns following are rotary cut, templates are included only when absolutely necessary.

Fabric preparation should be handled in the same manner that the quilt will be cared for when completed. I recommend prewashing all fabrics. As each piece enters my house, the first stop is the laundry room. All fabric in my personal stash has been washed using Orvus paste (a horse shampoo) or Dreft. Do not use detergent to wash your cotton fabrics because detergents act to strip color from cotton fabrics.

To replace the firmness of the sizing that has been washed out of the fabric, press all fabrics using a heavy spray starch. The fabric that is prepared in this way will behave much better when pressing seams, and bias edges will be more stable and less likely to stretch. You will find that piecing is much easier with fabric that doesn't stretch out of shape so quickly.

The yardages listed for each quilt pattern have been rounded up slightly to allow for the fact that "scrap" quilts tend to use more fabric than one would normally use. Multiple strips are used incompletely at times to create the greatest diversity in the fabric selection.

Yardage has been based upon 42" wide fabric. If your fabric is substantially wider or narrower after prewashing, your yardage requirement may also need adjustment.

The cutting instructions given for each pattern piece refer to the actual cut size. The 1/4" seam allowance has been added to all dimensions.

1/4" seams are used throughout the piecing. Check the accuracy of your seams before you begin. Accuracy is important to the success of your quilt. In the case of a quilt with a pieced border, the piecing of the body of the quilt will determine if the border fits properly! The measurements given are all mathematically correct, it is assumed that your piecing will also be correct.

Cutting instructions assume that all strips are cut the width of the fabric, measured selvage to selvage. This strip should measure 42" or longer. Do not cut the strip to this length.

Half square triangle units are made from layered fabric squares or rectangles using **triangle foundation papers**. The triangle foundation paper method allows for accurate results. Triangle foundation papers are available premade. Check with your local quilt shop for availability. Standard cutting instructions have been included for those who choose to construct half square triangles using traditional methods.

Specialty rulers are used to construct some patterns. Wherever appropriate, a brand name has been mentioned. Ask your local quilt shop if these rulers are available, or contact the manufacturer directly to purchase the ruler indicated. A template will also be given in these situations. I am a gadget person, if a ruler exists that will make my quilting easier, I will surely buy it!

Refer to the "Finishing" chapter for bordering questions. The quilts in this book were constructed using square borders. The **final border** on all quilts has been cut on the lengthwise grain of the fabric. The final border yardage reflects the lengthwise grain cut.

Pioneer Braid

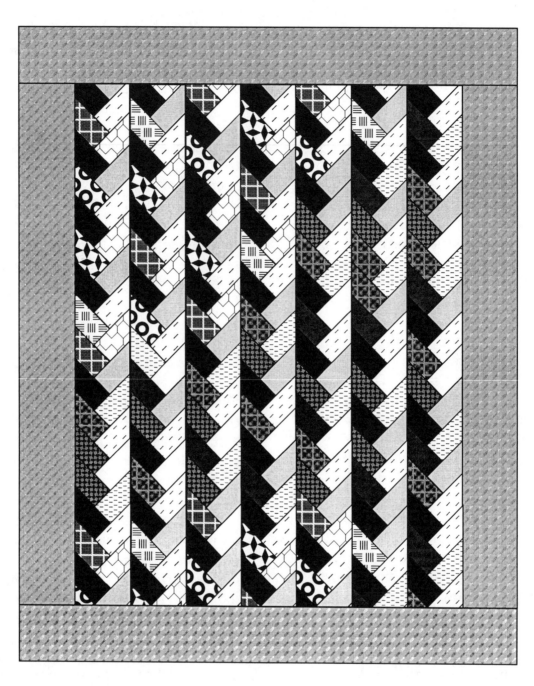

Fabric Requirements

	Lap Size 57" x 71"	Queen Size 96" x 106"	King Size 108" x 106"
Lights - assorted	1 1/2 yards	4 yards	4 1/2 yards
Darks - assorted	1 1/2 yards	4 yards	4 1/2 yards
Border - lengthwise cut	2 1/4 yards	3 1/2 yards	3 1/2 yards
Binding	3/4 yard	1 yard	1 yard
Backing	3 3/4 yards	9 yards	9 1/2 yards

Cutting Instructions

	Lap Size	Queen Size	King Size
Lights	16 strips 3" x 42"	48 strips 3" x 42"	50 strips 3" x 42"
Darks	16 strips 3" x 42"	48 strips 3" x 42"	50 strips 3" x 42"
Border - sides	2 - 6 1/2" x 61"	2 - 6 1/2" x 100"	2 - 6 1/2" x 112"
- top and bottom	2 - 6 1/2" x 63"	2 - 6 1/2" x 98"	2 - 6 1/2" x 98"

Strip Cutting

1. Unfold cut strips and layer several light strips right side up. Layer the fabric only as deep as you can accurately cut.

2. Trim off the selvages at the end of the strips. Place **Template A** at the trimmed end of the strips. Butt a ruler up to the diagonal edge of the template, remove the template, and cut along the edge of the ruler. Be sure to cut through all layers.

3. Rotate the template and place it onto the layered strip again. Butt the edge of a ruler against the straight edge of the template, remove the template and cut along the edge of the ruler. Continue this cutting method along the full length of the light fabric strips. Each fabric strip should yield 8 Template A pieces. Cut all light fabric strips in this manner.

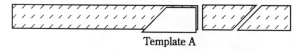

Template A

4. Layer several dark strips right sides up. Trim off the selvages at the end of the strip. Place **Template A-reverse** at the trimmed end of the strips. Cut along the diagonal edge.

5. Rotate the template and continue cutting Template A-reverse along the full length of the dark fabric strips.

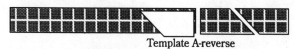

Template A-reverse

Braid Assembly

1. Stitch piece #1 (light) to a #2 (dark). Finger press the seam toward the bottom of the braid (#2).

2. Add piece #3 (light), finger press the seam toward the bottom of the braid (#3). Finger press the seams until you have added ten or more pieces. At that time you may press the seams using an iron. Because of the many bias edges, it is best to handle the strips carefully and not press the strip excessively or aggressively!

3. Continue to piece in this fashion until you have a very long strip.

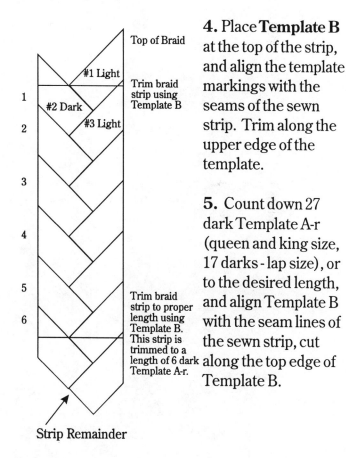

4. Place **Template B** at the top of the strip, and align the template markings with the seams of the sewn strip. Trim along the upper edge of the template.

5. Count down 27 dark Template A-r (queen and king size, 17 darks - lap size), or to the desired length, and align Template B with the seam lines of the sewn strip, cut along the top edge of Template B.

6. Continue adding pieces to the remainder of the original braid. Cut off lengths from this one braid until you have the desired number of vertical rows: king - 15, queen - 13, and lap - 7.

Quilt Top Assembly

1. Stitch rows together in pairs, pinning as needed. Stitch each pair together along one long edge. Handle carefully to prevent stretching. Press the long seam in one direction.

2. Join row pairs together forming the quilt top. Press the long seams in one direction.

3. Trim the final borders to fit and apply to the quilt top, attach the side borders first and then the top and bottom borders.

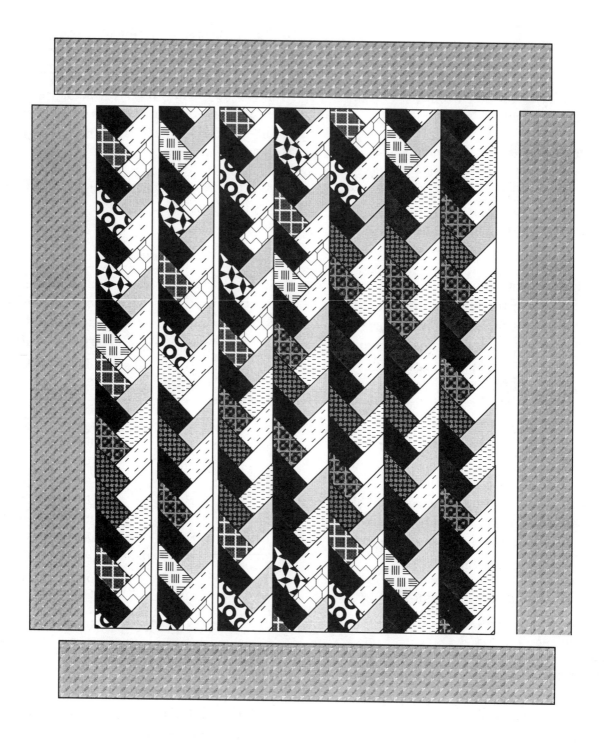

Broken Windmill

Fabric Requirements

	Lap	Double	Queen
	66" x 82 1/2"	82 1/2" x 99"	97 1/2" x 114"
	20 16 1/2" blocks	30 16 1/2" blocks	30 16 1/2" blocks
Background - Tan	4 1/4 yards	6 1/4 yards	6 1/4 yards
Main Color - Navy	1 1/2 yards	2 yards	2 yards
First Accent - Fuchsia	3/4 yard	1 yard	1 yard
Second Accent - Gold	3/4 yard	1 yard	1 yard
Pieced Border for Queen Size Quilt			
Dark Background			3 1/2 yards
Dark Fuchsia			3/4 yard
Dark Gold			3/4 yard
Binding	2/3 yard	3/4 yard	1 yard
Backing	4 yards	6 yards	9 yards

Cutting Instructions

	Lap	Double	Queen
Background			
2" strips	31	45	45
3 1/2" strips	22	33	33
Navy			
2" strips	17	26	26
5" strips	1	2	2
Gold			
2" strips	10	14	14
Fuchsia			
2" strips	10	14	14
Queen Pieced Border			
Dark Background			
8" strips			4
6 1/2" strips			3
5" strips			5
3 1/2" strips			5
2" strips			3
Dark Gold			
2" strips			4
3 1/2" strips			2
Dark Fuchsia			
2" strips			4
3 1/2" strips			2

Strip Piecing Instructions

1. Stitch 2" wide gold and fuchsia strips to 2" wide background strips as diagramed below. Use assorted fabric strips for the best variation. Press the seam toward the gold or fuchsia strip.

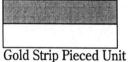 

Gold Strip Pieced Unit
Make Lap 6
Double/Queen 9

Fuchsia Strip Pieced Unit
Make Lap 6
Double/Queen 9

2. Subcut at 2" intervals to create rectangles.

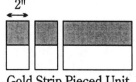 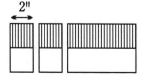

2"

2"

Gold Strip Pieced Unit
Cut Lap 120
Double/Queen 180

Fuchsia Strip Pieced Unit
Cut Lap 120
Double/Queen 180

3. Stitch pairs of gold/fuchsia and background 2" strips together as diagramed below. Press the seam toward the gold or fuchsia strip.

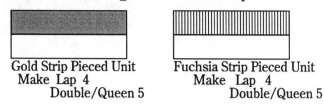

Gold Strip Pieced Unit
Make Lap 4
Double/Queen 5

Fuchsia Strip Pieced Unit
Make Lap 4
Double/Queen 5

4. Subcut at 3 1/2" intervals.

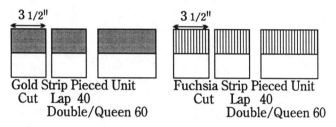

3 1/2"

3 1/2"

Gold Strip Pieced Unit
Cut Lap 40
Double/Queen 60

Fuchsia Strip Pieced Unit
Cut Lap 40
Double/Queen 60

5. Stitch a 2" wide navy strip to 2" and 3 1/2" wide background strips as diagramed below. Press the seams toward the navy strip. Subcut at 3 1/2" intervals.

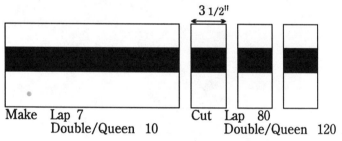

3 1/2"

Make Lap 7
Double/Queen 10

Cut Lap 80
Double/Queen 120

6. Stitch a 2" wide navy strip to a 3 1/2" wide background strip as diagramed below. Press the seam toward the navy strip. Subcut at 2" intervals to create rectangles.

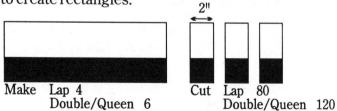

2"

Make Lap 4
Double/Queen 6

Cut Lap 80
Double/Queen 120

7. Cut 3 1/2" wide background strips into 3 1/2" squares.

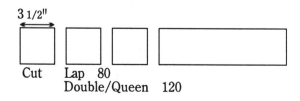

3 1/2"

Cut Lap 80
Double/Queen 120

8. Stitch 2" wide navy strips to 2" and 3 1/2" wide background strips as diagramed below. Press the seams toward the navy strips. Subcut at 2" intervals to create rectangles.

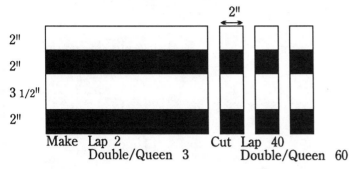

Make   Lap 2
        Double/Queen 3

Cut Lap 40
    Double/Queen 60

9. Stitch navy and background strips together as diagramed below. Press the seams toward the navy strips. Subcut at 2" intervals to create rectangles.

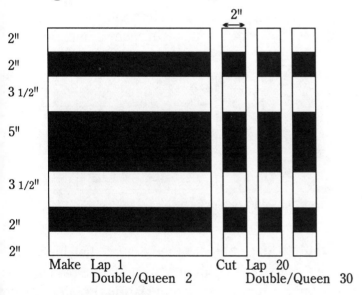

Make Lap 1
       Double/Queen 2

Cut Lap 20
    Double/Queen 30

Block Assembly

1. Assemble the units detailed above in steps 1 through 7 into rows. Be sure to keep the gold and the fuchsia fabrics segregated. Press the seams as indicated by the arrows.

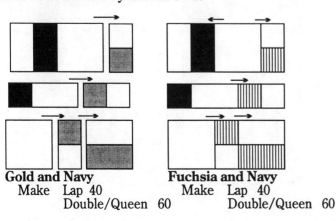

Gold and Navy
Make Lap 40
       Double/Queen 60

Fuchsia and Navy
Make Lap 40
       Double/Queen 60

2. Stitch rows together into quarter block pieces. Press the seams as diagramed. Each quarter block unit will measure 8" square

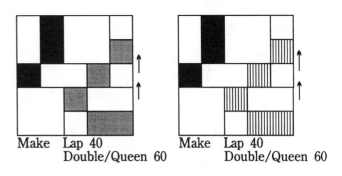

Make   Lap 40
    Double/Queen 60

Make   Lap 40
    Double/Queen 60

3. Stitch the quarter blocks and "sash" pieces together to form the completed block. Press the seams as indicated. The completed block will measure 17" square.

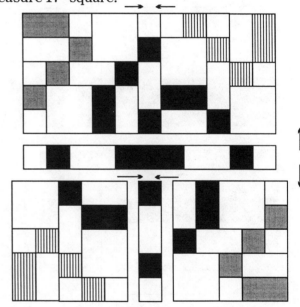

Make   Lap 20
    Double/Queen 30

Queen Pieced Border
- The pieced border will produce the added dimension to make the double bed size quilt into a queen bed size quilt.

Strip Piecing Instructions

1. Piece the strip units diagramed below. Press the seam toward the dark gold fabric. Subcut at 2" intervals.

Note each full strip should yield 21 units 2" wide. A total of 24 units 2" wide are required to complete the pieced border. Strip-piece an additional 9" wide segment of each combination to provide the extra length needed for the remaining 3 units 2" wide. Strips have been cut to allow for this additional piecing.

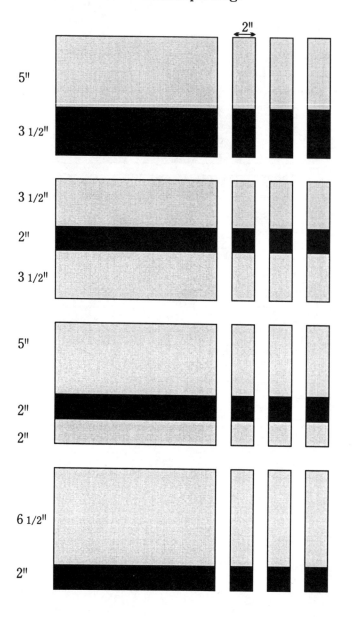

2. Repeat the piecing detailed at left using the dark fuchsia strips. Subcut each into 24 units.

3. Subcut the 8" wide dark background strips into 70 rectangles 2" wide.

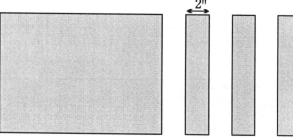

Cut 8" strips into 70 rectangles

4. Arrange the subcut units into border quarter blocks. Press the seams as indicated by the arrows. The completed squares will measure 8" square. Set aside 2 squares of each color family.

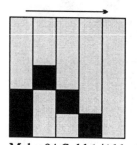 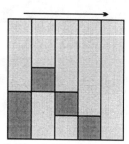

Make 24 Gold 1/4 blocks   Make 24 Fuchsia 1/4 blocks

5. Stitch quarter blocks together into half block units. Separate the squares with a 2" x 8" wide rectangle of dark background fabric. Press.

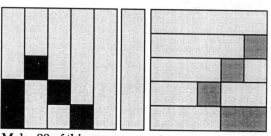

Make 22 of this arrangement

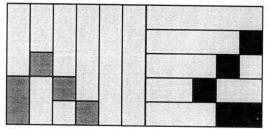

Make 22 of this arrangement

Quilt Top Assembly

1. Join the blocks together into rows: lap - 4 x 5; and double/queen - 5 x 6. Alternate the fuchsia and gold corners to create a secondary pattern of gold and fuchsia windmills.

2. The lap and double size quilt piecing is complete at this point. You may add a plain border if you wish before the quilt is finished.

Queen Pieced Border

3. Arrange half and quarter blocks to form border strips. Attach borders and press.

4. Refer to the general finishing directions in chapter 6. Layer, quilt, bind and enjoy your new quilt.

Tablescraps

Fabric Requirements

	Wall Hanging	**Twin**	**Queen**
	64" x 64"	64" x 88"	88" x 112"
	16 12" blocks	24 12" blocks	48 12" blocks
Background	5 yards - white	4 1/2 yards - dark	8 1/2 yards - dark
Stars and Chains	2 yards - navy	3 yards - lights	5 yards - lights
Border	included in background	3 yards	3 1/2 yards
Binding	3/4 yard	3/4 yard	included in border
Backing	4 yards	5 1/2 yards	8 yards

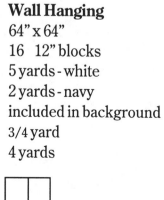

Cutting Instructions

NOTE Each block requires one 6 1/4" x 15" rectangle of background fabric, four 4 1/2" squares of the matching background fabric, and one rectangle 6 1/4" x 15" of "stars and chains" fabric. Please cut your fabric accordingly.

	1 Block	Wall Hanging	Twin	Queen
Border - cut first and set aside, lengthwise grain cut				
- sides		2 - 4 1/2" x 60"	2 - 4 1/2" x 84"	2 - 4 1/2" x 108"
- top and bottom		2 - 4 1/2" x 68"	2 - 4 1/2" x 68"	2 - 4 1/2" x 92"
Pieced Border				
4 1/2" x 8 1/2" rectangle		16	20	28
6 1/4" square		3	3	4
Background				
6 1/4" x 15" rectangle	1	16	24	48
4 1/2" square	4	64	96	192
Pieced Border				
6 1/4" squares		8	9	12
Stars and Chains				
6 1/4" x 15" rectangle	1	16	24	48
Pieced Border				
2 1/2" square		16	20	28
6 1/4" squares		11	12	16

Block Construction

NOTE The fabrics have been cut to allow for the use of triangle foundation papers when constructing half square triangles. If you wish to piece the triangles in the traditional method (triangle to triangle), cut each 6 1/4" x 15" rectangle into ten 2 7/8" squares and cut each 2 7/8" square once diagonally. Each rectangle will produce 20 half square triangles 2 7/8".

1. Photocopy or trace the number of triangle foundation papers necessary for your chosen quilt. The paper used will be five squares long and two squares wide. The original foundation included in this book is 3 x 2. Trace two additional rows of squares and attach to the end of the paper before you begin to photocopy so that your grid is the correct size.

> **Copy** Wallhanging 16
> Twin 24
> Queen 48

2. Using a 6 1/4" x 15" rectangle of background fabric, and a rectangle of stars and chains fabric, construct half square triangle units using the triangle foundation paper method detailed on page 15. Each rectangle pair will yield 20 2 1/2" half square triangles, enough to construct one block.

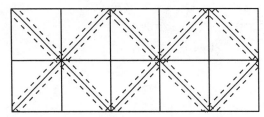

3. For each block, stitch the 20 half square triangle units together to create 5 broken dishes units. Press the seams as diagramed below.

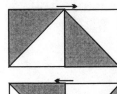
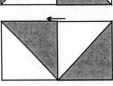
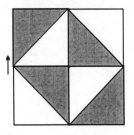

4. Using the broken dishes components from step 3 and the 4 matching 4 1/2" squares of background fabric, assemble the blocks as shown below. Press the seams as diagramed.

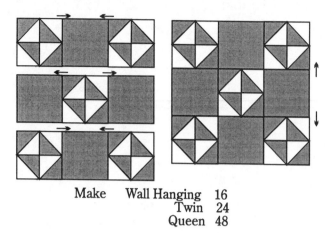

Make   Wall Hanging   16
Twin   24
Queen   48

Pieced Border

Pieced Border - The pieced border consists of two "half" blocks. One being the mirror image of the other.

NOTE The fabrics have been cut to allow for the use of triangle foundation papers. If you wish to bypass the use of the papers, cut each 6 1/4" square into four 2 7/8" squares, and cut each square once diagonally. Each 6 1/4" square will produce eight half square triangles 2 7/8".

1. Photocopy or trace triangle foundation papers necessary for your project. The paper used will be two squares long x two squares wide.

Copy   Wallhanging   11
Twin   12
Queen   16

2. Using the 6 1/4" squares of fabric specified for the pieced border, construct half square triangles using the triangle foundation paper method detailed on page 15. Pair each square of background or border fabric with a square of stars and chains fabric. Each square will yield eight half square triangle units measuring 2 1/2".

3. Piece the broken dishes components necessary for the pieced border half blocks. Place the border fabric in each broken dishes unit as diagramed. When the border fabric is placed in this way, it creates the illusion that the stars flow out from the body of the pieced quilt and are framed by the border.

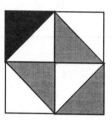

Make

Wall Hanging   20
Twin   24
Queen   32

4. Stitch the broken dishes component to the 4 1/2" x 8 1/2" border fabric rectangle. The four remaining broken dishes units will be the corners of the pieced border assembly.

Make   Wall Hanging   8 of each unit
Twin   10 of each unit
Queen   14 of each unit

5. Position a 2 1/2" square of stars and chains fabric on the corner of the border fabric rectangle. Align the raw edges, stitch across the square from point to point. Trim the excess fabric to a 1/4" seam allowance and press.

Quilt Top Assembly

1. Assemble the blocks into rows, and sew the rows together to form the quilt top: wall hanging - 4 x 4; twin - 4 x 6; and queen - 6 x 8. Notice that all of the numbers are even numbers. This ensures that the secondary pattern created as the blocks intersect will be a completed pattern.

2. Lay out the pieced border half blocks and stitch together into strips and apply to the body of the quilt. Press the seam toward the border strips.

3. Trim the final borders to fit and apply to the quilt top, attach the side borders first and then the top and bottom borders. Press all seams toward the border strips.

Friendship Star

Fabric Requirements

	Lap	Twin	King
	60" x 78"	78" x 87"	108" x 117"
	35 9" blocks	56 9" blocks	110 9" blocks
Background	2 yards	3 1/4 yards	5 3/8 yards
Stars - Dark	2 1/4 yards	3 3/4 yards	6 1/2 yards
First Border	1/2 yard	3/4 yard	3/4 yard
Final Border	2 1/4 yards	2 3/4 yards	3 1/2 yards
Binding	3/4 yard	1 yard	1 yard
Backing	4 yards	5 1/4 yards	10 yards

Cutting Instructions

	1 Block	Lap	Twin	King
Background				
8 1/4" square	1	35	56	110
Stars - Dark				
8 1/4" square	1	35	56	110
3 1/2" square	1	35	56	110
First Border				
2" wide strips		6	7	10
Final Border - sides		2 - 6 1/2" x 70"	2 - 6 1/2" x 80"	2 - 7 1/2" x 106"
- top and bottom		2 - 6 1/2" x 64"	2 - 6 1/2" x 82"	2 - 7 1/2" x 111"
Binding				
2 1/2" strips		7	9	12

Block Construction

NOTE The fabrics have been cut to allow for the use of triangle foundation papers when constructing half square triangles. If you wish to piece the triangles in the traditional method (triangle to triangle), cut each 8 1/4" square into four 3 7/8" squares and cut each 3 7/8" square once diagonally. Each rectangle will produce eight half square triangles 3 7/8".

1. Photocopy or trace the number of triangle foundation papers necessary for your chosen quilt. The paper used will be two squares long x two squares wide.

Copy	Lap	35
	Twin	56
	King	110

2. Place an 8 1/4" square of background fabric right sides together with an 8 1/4" square of star fabric. Construct half square triangles following the triangle foundation paper method detailed on page 15. Each square pair will yield eight half square triangle units measuring 3 1/2".

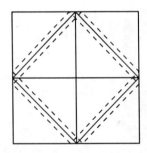

3. Select and arrange nine half square units as diagramed below. The plain center square and four of the half square triangles should contain the same fabric. These matching colored squares will make up the star. The remaining four half square triangles should all be different for the greatest variety possible. Press the seams as diagramed.

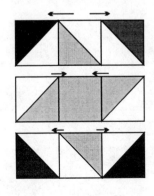 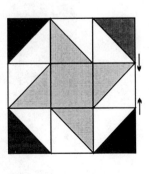

Quilt Top Assembly

1. Assemble the blocks into rows, and sew the rows together to form the quilt top: lap - 5 x 7; twin - 7 x 8; king - 10 x 11. Rotate each block to create opposing seam allowances.

2. Diagonally piece the first border strips together, cut lengths as needed, and apply to the quilt. Press the seams toward the border strip.

3. Trim final borders to fit and apply to the quilt top, attach the side borders first and then the top and bottom borders. Press all seams toward the border strips.

Road to Oklahoma

Fabric Requirements

	Lap 60" x 76"	Double 76" x 92"	Queen 92" x 108"
Background	3 3/4 yards	4 3/4 yards	6 1/2 yards
Gold - Chain	3/4 yard	1 1/4 yards	1 1/2 yards
Red - Chain	3/4 yard	1 1/4 yards	1 1/2 yards
Stars and **Pieced Border**	2 1/4 yards	3 1/2 yards	4 1/2 yards
First Border	3/4 yard	3/4 yard	1 yard
Binding	3/4 yard	3/4 yard	7/8 yard
Backing	3 3/4 yards	5 1/2 yards	8 1/4 yards

Cutting Instructions

	Lap	Double	Queen
Background			
4 Patch Chains			
2 1/2" strips	12	20	30
Star Units			
2 1/2" squares	96	160	240
6 1/4" squares	24	40	60
Pieced Border			
2 1/2" strips	9	11	13
Gold			
4 Patch Chains			
2 1/2" strips	6	10	15
Red			
4 Patch Chains			
2 1/2" strips	6	10	15

Stars and Pieced Border

The star fabrics were cut to create complete stars. If this is how you would like to color the stars, each complete star will require 4 squares 2 1/2" and one square 6 1/4". Cut your fabric accordingly.

	Lap	Double	Queen
Stars			
2 1/2" squares	96	160	240
6 1/4" squares	24	40	60
Pieced Border			
2 1/2" strips	9	11	13
First Border			
2 1/2" strips	6	7	9
Binding			
2 1/2" strips	7	8	10

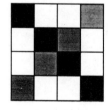  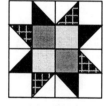 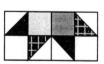

Block A   Half Block A-1   Half Block A-2   Block B   Half Block B   Corner

Finished block size: 8" x 8"

	Lap	Double	Queen
Block A	17	31	49
Half Block A-1	8	10	12
Half Block A-2	6	8	10
Block B	18	32	50
Half Block B	10	14	18
Corner Block	4	4	4

Block A Assembly

Four Patch Units

1. Stitch each 2 1/2"-wide red strip to a 2 1/2"-wide background strip along the long edge. Press the seam toward the red strip. Repeat with all 2 1/2"-wide red strips.

2. Place two sets of sewn red strips right sides together, reversing the colors as shown in the diagram. The seam allowances will be opposing.

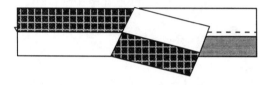

3. Trim the selvage from the strip ends. Cut the strip pairs into 2 1/2" pairs.

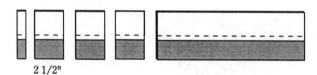

2 1/2"

4. Chain piece the subcut pairs. The pairs are cut with the seam allowances aligned and ready for stitching. Stitch with the background fabric placed as shown (this will be important later for opposing seams). Press the seam to one side.

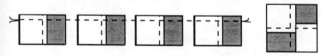

5. Repeat instructions 1 - 4 using gold and background strips to make gold Four Patches.

Block Construction

1. Stitch gold four patch units to red four patch units as diagramed. Watch the placement of the seam allowances very closely. Press the seam toward the gold four patch.

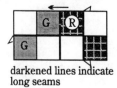

darkened lines indicate long seams

Make
Lap - 42 sets
Double - 72 sets
Queen - 110 sets

Set aside joined four patches and label them as Half Block A-1: Lap - 8, Double - 10, and Queen - 12.

2. Join remaining units from step 1 to form completed Block A's. After the long seam is stitched, pull the two or three stitches of the vertical seam that extend past the long seam into the 1/4" seam allowance. This will allow the final seam to be swirled and pressed so that all of the seams are rotating in the same direction, distributing the bulk in the center of the block.

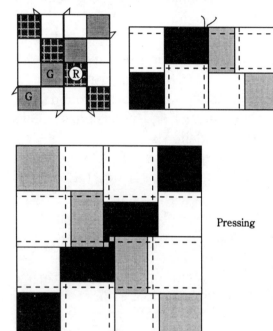

Pressing

3. Stitch remaining gold and red four patch units as diagramed. Watch the placement of the seam allowances very closely. Press the seam toward the red four patch.

darkened lines indicate long seams

Make
Lap - 6
Double - 8
Queen - 10

Set aside joined four patches and label them as Half Block A-2.

Block B Assembly

NOTE The fabrics have been cut to allow for the use of triangle foundation papers when constructing half square triangles. If you wish to piece the triangles in the traditional method (triangle to triangle), cut each 6 1/4" square into four 2 7/8" squares and cut each 2 7/8" square once diagonally. Each 6 1/4" square will produce eight half square triangles 2 7/8"

1. Photocopy or trace the number of triangle foundation papers necessary for your chosen quilt. The paper used will be two squares long x two squares wide.

Copy	Lap	24
	Double	40
	Queen	60

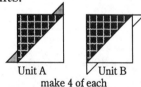

2. Place each 6 1/4" square of star fabric right sides together with a 6 1/4" square of background fabric, with the background fabric on top. Construct half square triangles following the triangle foundation paper method detailed on page 15. Each square pair will yield eight half square triangle units measuring 2 1/2".

3. Separate each set of 8 half square triangles into two sets of four. Press the seams of one set of four toward the star fabric, these will be the A units. Press the seams of the second set of four toward the background fabric, these will be the B units.

Unit A   Unit B
make 4 of each

Make Lap - 192
Double - 320
Queen - 480

Half will be A units, half B units.

4. Remove the paper foundation. Place your thumb nail on the stitched seam at the center of the block. Pull the paper foundation from the square corner against your thumb nail. This will help to reduce the number of stitches lost at the seam ends. Trim all dog ears.

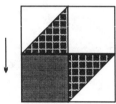

Unit A   Unit B

Block Construction

1. To each B triangle square, stitch a 2 1/2" square of background fabric. Press the seam toward the triangle square.

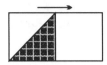

2. To each A triangle square, stitch a 2 1/2" square of star fabric. Press the seam toward the triangle square.

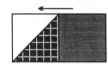

3. Stitch each unit from step 1 to a unit from step 2. Press the seam toward the dark unit as diagramed.

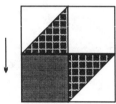

Make
Lap - 96
Double - 160
Queen - 240

Set aside 4 quarter star units and label them as Corner Blocks.

4. Stitch quarter star units from step 3 together into block half. Press the seam as indicated in the diagram.

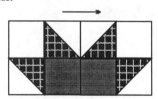

Set aside half star blocks and label them as Half Block B: Lap - 10, Double - 14, and Queen - 18.

5. Join remaining half star blocks together to form completed Block B's. Release the last two stitches of the vertical seams and swirl the seam allowance of the final long seam, as diagramed for the chain block.

Pieced Border Construction

1. Stitch each 2 1/2"-wide colored strip to a 2 1/2"-wide background strip along the long edge. Press the seam toward the colored strip. Repeat with all pieced border strips.

2. Order strip pairs from step 1 in a pleasing color arrangement. Stitch strip pairs together into larger strip unit. Press all seams toward the colored strips.

3. Straighten the strip end. Cut the strip units into 2 1/2" segments.

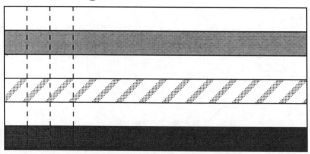

cut into 2 1/2" segments

4. Stitch the 2 1/2" segments together into long chains. "Break" the long chain apart between squares, by removing stitches, to create strips of the correct length to border your quilt. Make 4 strips of the length specified for your side borders and 4 strips for the top and bottom borders.

Side Borders:
Lap - 17 color and 17 background squares
Double - 21 color and 21 background squares
Queen - 26 color and 26 background squares

Top and Bottom Borders:
Lap - 15 color and 15 background squares
Double - 19 color and 19 background squares
Queen - 23 color and 23 background squares

5. Stitch strips into pairs. Alternate the placement of the colored and background squares to create a checkerboard effect.

Quilt Top Assembly

1. Arrange blocks, half blocks, and corner blocks on your floor or design wall. Turn the chain blocks so that continuous red and gold chains run diagonally across the quilt. The half blocks and corner blocks complete the design.

Lap Size Quilt diagramed

NOTE in the diagram above, the heavy lines indicate the placement of the blocks, half blocks, and corner blocks. When arranging the blocks, the corner blocks will all be complete stars, and the corners are quarter star units.

    Lap: 7 rows x 5 blocks
    Double: 9 rows x 7 blocks
    Queen: 11 rows x 9 blocks

2. Add the 2 1/2"-wide border strips. Press the seams toward the border strips.

3. Add the pieced border strips. Add the side borders first. Press the seams toward the first border.

Road to Oklahoma   37

Corn and Beans

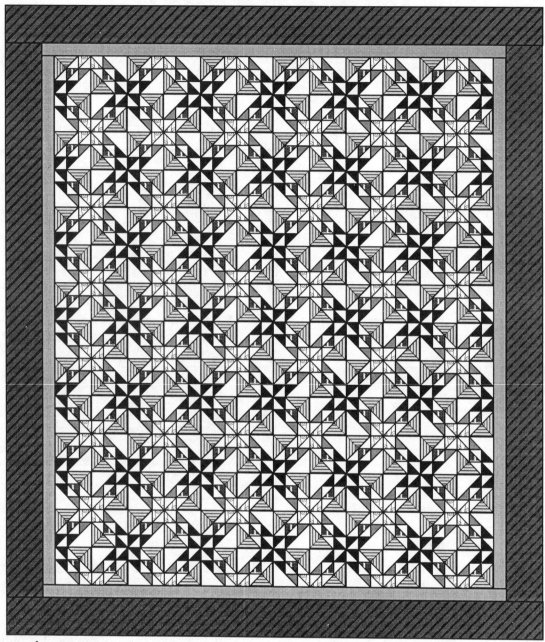

Fabric Requirements

	Twin	Queen
	64" x 88"	88" x 100"
	24 12" blocks	42 12" blocks
Assorted Lights	3 yards	5 yards
Assorted Darks	3 yards	5 yards
First Border	3/4 yard	3/4 yard
Final Border	2 1/2 yards	3 yards
Binding	3/4 yard	1 yard
Backing	5 1/2 yards	8 yards

Cutting Instructions

	1 Block	Twin	Queen
Assorted Lights			
2 7/8" square	4	96	168
4 7/8" square	2	48	84
6 1/4" square	1 1/2	36	63
Assorted Darks			
2 7/8" square	4	96	168
4 7/8" square	2	48	84
6 1/4" square	1 1/2	36	63
First Border			
2 1/2" strips		7	8
Final Border - sides		2 - 6 1/2" x 80"	2 - 6 1/2" x 94
- top and bottom		2 - 6 1/2" x 68"	2 - 6 1/2" x 92"
Binding			
2 1/2" strips		8	10

Block Construction

NOTE The fabrics have been cut to allow for the use of triangle foundation papers when constructing half square triangles. If you wish to piece the triangles in the traditional method (triangle to triangle), cut each 6 1/4" square into four 2 7/8" squares and cut each 2 7/8" square once diagonally. Each square will produce eight half square triangles 2 7/8".

1. Photocopy or trace the number of triangle foundation papers necessary for your chosen quilt. The paper used will be two squares long x two squares wide.

Copy	Twin	36
	Queen	63

2. Place a 6 1/4" square of light fabric right sides together with a 6 1/4" square of dark fabric. Construct half square triangles following the triangle foundation paper method detailed on page 15. Each square pair will yield eight half square triangle units measuring 2 1/2".

3. Cut each 2 7/8" square in half once diagonally.

4. To one third of the half square triangle units attach a dark 2 7/8" triangle. Press the seam toward the dark triangle.

Make Twin 96
Queen 168

5. To one third of the half square triangle units attach one dark and one light 2 7/8" triangle. Press the seams as diagramed.

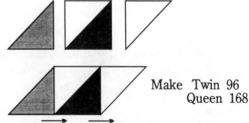

Make Twin 96
Queen 168

6. To the remaining half square triangle units attach a light 2 7/8" triangle. Press the seam as diagramed below.

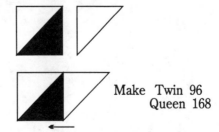

Make Twin 96
Queen 168

7. Join units from steps 4, 5, and 6 together. Press the seams in one direction.

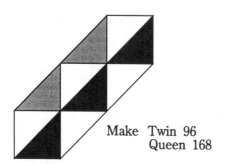

Make Twin 96
Queen 168

8. Cut each 4 7/8" square in half once diagonally.

9. Stitch a 4 7/8" triangle to each long edge of the unit from step 6. Use one light triangle and one dark triangle. Place colors as diagramed below. Press as indicated by the arrows. Each square should measure 6 1/2".

Make Twin 96
Queen 168

10. To simplify the construction of the quilt top, stitch the squares together in groups of four as diagramed below. Press the seams as indicated by the arrows.

Quilt Top Assembly

1. Stitch the quilt top into rows, and sew the rows together to form the quilt top: twin - 4 x 6; queen - 6 x 7.

2. Diagonally piece the first border strips together, cut lengths as needed, and apply to the quilt. Press the seams toward the border strip.

3. Trim the final borders to fit and apply to the quilt top, attach side borders first and then the top and bottom borders. Press all seams toward the border strips.

Pioneer Braid, by Brenda Henning, 1997; Anchorage, AK; 108"x106".
Quilted by Norma Kindred. Collection of William C. Buchwald. Photo: Ken Wagner.

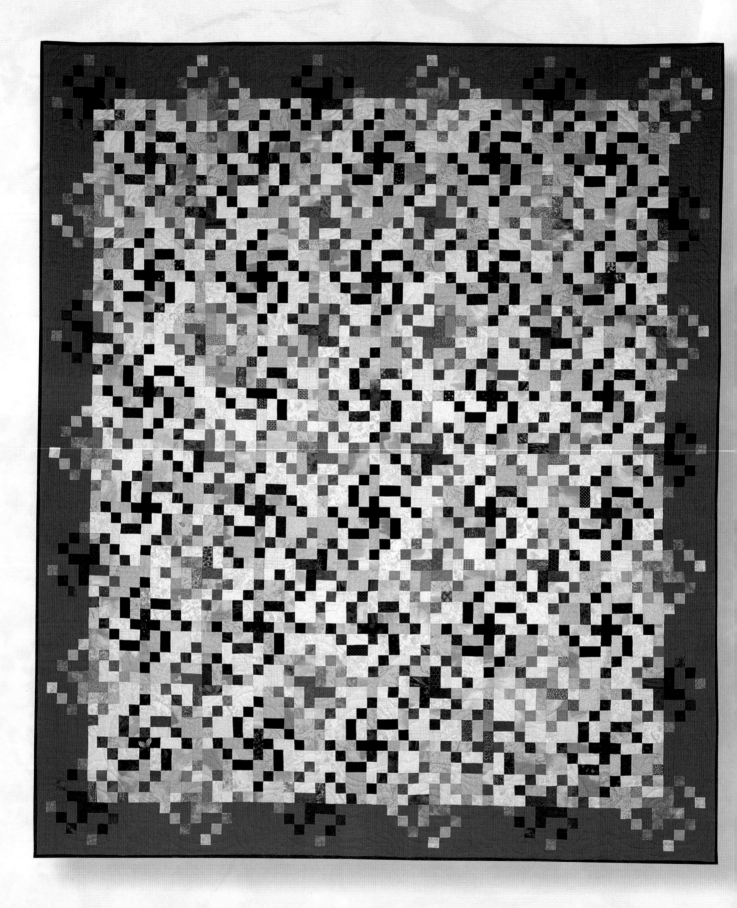

Broken Windmill, by Brenda Henning, with help of the Material Girls and the Sourdough Stitchers, 1997; Anchorage, AK; 971/2"x114". Quilted by Norma Kindred. Photo: Mark Frey.

Tablescraps (left), by Brenda Henning, 1995; Anchorage, AK; 64"x64". Quilted by Norma Kindred. Photo: Mark Frey.

Tablescraps (below), by Brenda Henning, 1995; Anchorage, AK; 88"x112". Quilted by Norma Kindred. Photo: Ken Wagner.

Friendship Star, by Kathryn Rhea, 1997; Anchorage, AK; 108"x117".
Quilted by Norma Kindred. Collection of Edward C. Mould. Photo: Mark Frey.

Road to Oklahoma, by Brenda Henning, 1997; Anchorage, AK; 76"x92".
Quilted by Norma Kindred. Photo: Mark Frey.

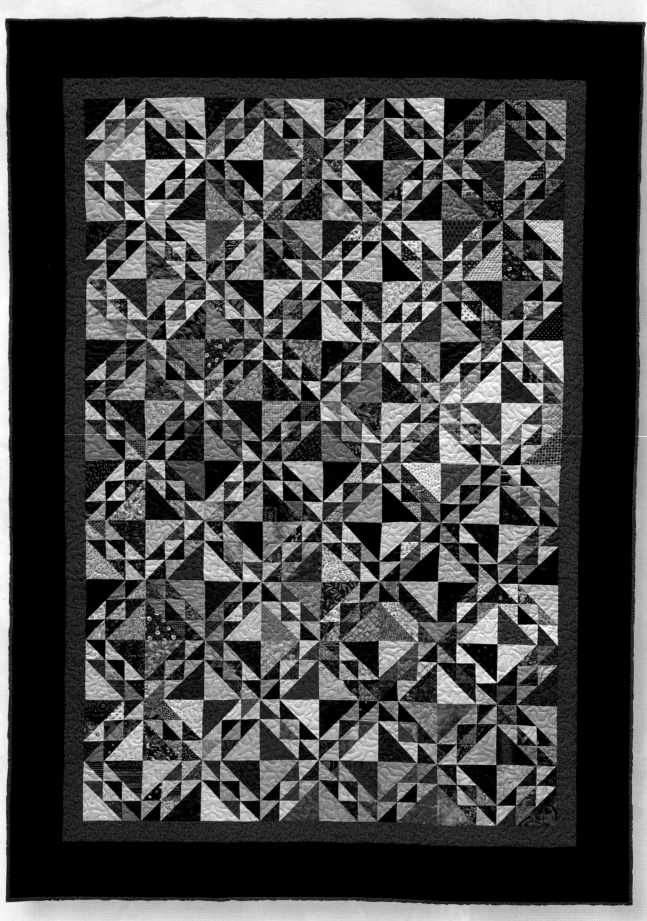

Corn and Beans, by Debbie Repasky, with help from the Material Girls and the Sourdough Stitchers, 1996; Anchorage, AK; 64"x88". Quilted by Brenda Harris. Photo: Ken Wagner.

Cabin Fever Bears, by Brenda Henning, with help from the Material Girls and the Sourdough Stitchers, 1995; Anchorage, AK; 85"x102". Quilted by Brenda Harris. Photo: Mark Frey.

Falling Leaves, by Brenda Henning, 1997; Anchorage, AK; 92"x108".
Quilted by Norma Kindred. Photo: Mark Frey.

Autograph Lattice, by Brenda Henning, 1997; Anchorage, AK; 41"x51".
Quilted by Norma Kindred. Photo: Mark Frey.

All A Twinkle, by Brenda Henning, 1994; Anchorage, AK; 90"x102".
Photo: Mark Frey.

Whirligig (left), by Brenda Henning, 1994; Anchorage, AK; 90"x102". Quilted by Norma Kindred. Photo: Ken Wagner.

Whirligig (below), by Brenda Henning, with help from the Sourdough Stitchers, 1996; Anchorage, AK; 80"x96". Quilted by Norma Kindred. Photo: Mark Frey.

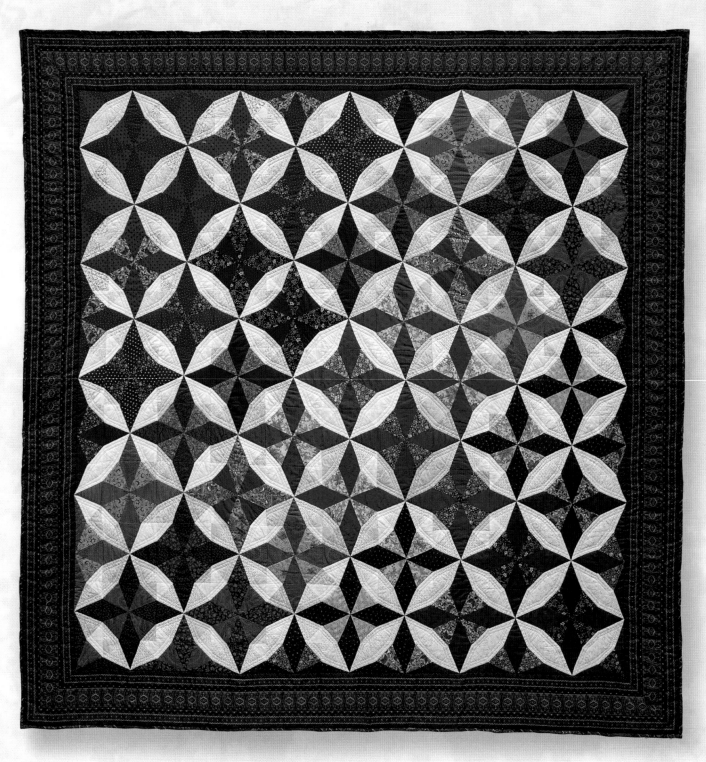

Kaleidoscope, by Brenda Henning, 1994; Anchorage, AK; 72"x72".
Photo: Ken Wagner.

Cabin Fever Bears

Fabric Requirements

	Wall Hanging	Queen
	51" square	85" x 102"
	4 14" blocks	20 14"blocks
Background	2 yards	6 yards
Assorted Darks		
Claws and Paw Pads	1 1/4 yards	4 yards
Medium - 1 Fabric		
Paw Pads	1/2 yard	2 yards
Border	1 1/2 yards	2 3/4 yards
Binding	3/4 yard	1 yard
Backing	3 1/4 yards	7 3/4 yards

Cutting Instructions

	1 Block	Wall Hanging	Queen
Background			
Full Size Bear Paw Blocks			
2 1/2" square	4	16	80
2 1/2" x 6 1/2"	4	16	80
6 1/4" square	2	8	40
Miniature Bear Paws			
1 1/2" square		5	16
4 1/4" square		3	8
Sashing			
3 1/2" x 14 1/2"		4	31
First Border			
3 1/2" strips		4	8
Assorted Darks			
Full Size Bear Paw Blocks			
Paw Pads - parenthetical number indicates piecing order			
(2) 1" square	4	16	80
(3) 1" x 1 1/2"	4	16	80
(6) 1" x 2"	4	16	80
(7) 1" x 2 1/2"	4	16	80
(10) 1" x 3"	4	16	80
(11) 1" x 3 1/2"	4	16	80
(14) 1" x 4"	4	16	80
(15) 1" x 4 1/2"	4	16	80
Claws 6 1/4" square	2	8	40
Center Square 2 1/2" square	1	4	20
Miniature Bear Paws			
Miniature Claws 4 1/4" square		3	8
Miniature Paw Pads - these will be paper pieced - cut assorted strips 1" wide.			
Medium - single fabric used			
Full Size Bear Paw Blocks			
(1) 1" square - center	4	16	80
(4) 1" x 1 1/2"	4	16	80
(5) 1" x 2"	4	16	80
(8) 1" x 2 1/2"	4	16	80
(9) 1" x 3"	4	16	80
(12) 1" x 3 1/2"	4	16	80
(13) 1" x 4"	4	16	80
Miniature Paw Pads - these will be paper pieced - cut strips 1" wide.			
Border - lengthwise cut			
- sides		2 - 7 1/2" x 42"	2 - 7 1/2" x 92"
- top and bottom		2 - 7 1/2" x 55"	2 - 7 1/2" x 92"
Binding			
2 1/2" strips		6	10

Piecing and Assembly

Log Cabin Construction

NOTE Accuracy is very important to the success of a log cabin project.
- All logs have been cut to the correct size. If stitched correctly, there will be no excess strip, and there will be no need to stretch the log to fit.
- If you are having difficulty making the logs fit:
    a) double check your seam allowance; and
    b) double check your cutting accuracy.

1. Stitch all (1) and (2) 1" squares together. Chain piece as you stitch the log cabin units to save time and thread. Press the seam toward the (2) square, which is dark.

2. Stitch all (3) rectangles to the unit from step 1 above. Press the seam toward the (3) rectangle.

3. Continue adding rectangles to the log cabin in the order listed in the cutting directions. Press all seams toward the outer edge of the block.

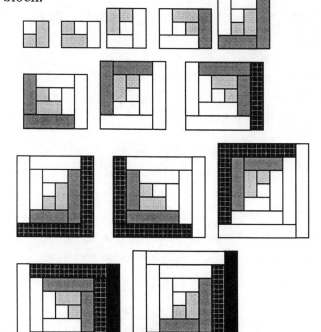

Claw Construction

NOTE The fabrics have been cut to allow for the use of triangle foundation papers when constructing half square triangles. If you wish to piece the triangles in the traditional method (triangle to triangle), cut each 6 1/4" square into four 2 7/8" squares and cut each 2 7/8" square once diagonally. Each square will produce eight half square triangles 2 7/8". Cut each 4 1/4" square (miniature paws) into four 1 7/8" squares and cut each 1 7/8" square once diagonally. Each square will produce eight half square triangles 1 7/8".

1. Photocopy or trace the number of triangle foundation papers necessary for your chosen quilt. The paper used will be two squares long x two squares wide.

Copy		Blocks	Mini-paws
	Wall Hanging	8	3
	Queen	40	8

2. Place a 6 1/4" square of background fabric right sides together with a 6 1/4" square of dark fabric. Construct half square triangles following the triangle foundation paper method detailed on page 15. Each square pair will yield eight half square triangle units measuring 2 1/2".

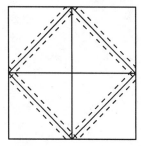

3. Place an 4 1/4" square of background fabric right sides together with an 4 1/4" square of dark fabric. Construct half square triangles following the triangle foundation paper method detailed on page 15. Each square pair will yield eight half square triangle units measuring 1 1/2".

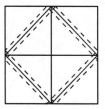

55

Full Size Bear Paw Construction

1. Stitch half square triangle units together as diagramed below. Four such units are required to complete each block. Press the seam toward the dark fabric.

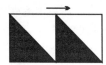

Make Wallhanging 16
      Queen   80

2. Stitch half square triangle units together as diagramed below, to one end add a 2 1/2" square of background fabric. Four such units are required to complete each block. Press the seams as indicated by the arrows. Notice that the triangles are arranged differently than those joined in step 1.

Make Wallhanging 16
      Queen   80

3. Join half square units from steps 1 and 2 to log cabin blocks. Press the seams toward the log cabin block. Four units are required to complete each block.

4. Complete construction of the log cabin blocks. Press the seams as indicated in the diagram. Press the long final seams toward the "sashing" strip.

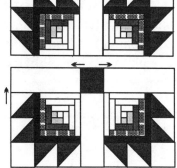

2 1/2" x 6 1/2"
stitched to
2 1/2" square

Miniature Bear Paw Construction

NOTE If you prefer, a 3 1/2" square of dark fabric can be substituted for the pieced miniature bear paw.

1. Photocopy or trace the miniature bear paw pad template below.

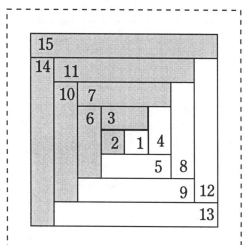

Make

Wall Hanging 5
Queen   16

2. Paper piece the miniature bear paw pad using the 1" wide strips of the medium fabric and the assorted dark strips. Follow the paper piecing directions given on page 15.

3. Trim the pieced unit on the dotted line, this will leave a 1/4" seam allowance at the edge of the miniature pad.

4. Remove the foundation paper from the back of the design.

5. Stitch half square triangles units together as diagramed below. Press the seam toward the dark fabric triangle.

Make Wallhanging 5
      Queen   16

6. Stitch half square triangle units together as diagramed below, to one end add a 1 1/2" square of background fabric. Press the seams as indicated by the arrows. Notice that the triangles are arranged differently than those joined in step 5.

Make Wallhanging 5
      Queen   16

7. Join half square triangle units from steps 5 and 6 to the miniature log cabin blocks. Press the seams toward the log cabin.

Quilt Top Assembly

1. Join blocks and sashing strips together into rows. Press all seams toward sashing strips.

2. Join remaining sashing strips and miniature bear paw blocks together into rows. Press all seams toward the sashing strips.

3. Assemble rows of blocks with rows of sashing between them. Press the long seams toward the sashing strips.

4. Diagonally piece the first border strips together, cut lengths as needed. Attach the first border, using the four remaining miniature blocks as corner posts. Press all seams toward the border strips.

5. Trim final borders to fit and apply to the quilt top, attach side borders first and then the top and bottom border strips. Press all seams toward the final border.

Falling Leaves

Fabric Requirements

	Lap 64" x 80 48 8" blocks	Double 80" x 96 80 8" blocks	Queen 92" x 108" 80 8" blocks **plus** **Pieced Border**
Background	3 yards	3 3/4 yards	6 yards
Leaf Tips	1 1/4 yards	2 1/4 yards	3 1/2 yards
Leaf Body	1 1/2 yards	2 1/4 yards	3 1/2 yards
Leaf Stem	1/2 yard	3/4 yard	3/4 yard
First Border	3/4 yard	1 yard	1 yard
Final Border	2 1/4 yards	2 3/4 yards	3 1/4 yards
Binding	3/4 yard	3/4 yard	1 yard
Backing	4 1/4 yards	6 yards	8 1/2 yards

Cutting Instructions

	1 block	Lap	Double	Queen
Background Fabric				
A - 2 1/2" square	1	48	80	80
B - 6 1/4" x 9" rectangle	1/2	24	40	40
C - 4 1/4" square	1	48	80	80
Leaf Tips				
D - 6 1/4" x 9" rectangle	1/2	24	40	40
Leaf Bodies*				
E - 3" x 4" rectangle	1	48	80	80
F - 3" x 6 1/2" rectangle	1	48	80	80
NOTE Each 3" x 4" leaf piece needs a matching 3" x 6 1/2" piece.				
Leaf Stem				
G - 7 1/4" x 1 1/4" rectangle	1	48	80	80
First Border				
2 1/2" strips		5 strips	8 strips	8 strips
Final Border - sides		2 - 6 1/2" x 72"	2 - 6 1/2" x 88"	2 - 4 1/2" x 104"
- top and bottom		2 - 6 1/2" x 68"	2 - 6 1/2" x 84"	2 - 4 1/2" x 96"
Binding				
2 1/2" strips		8	9	10

Tumbling Triangles Border - Queen Size Only

Background Fabric

6 1/4" squares	38
4 7/8" squares	42
5 1/4" square	1

Colored Fabrics
- using Leaf Tip and Leaf Body Remnants

6 1/4" squares	38
4 7/8" squares	44
5 1/4" square	1

Leaf Tip Construction

NOTE The fabrics have been cut to allow for the use of triangle foundation papers when constructing half square triangles. If you wish to piece the triangles in the traditional method (triangle to triangle), cut each 6 1/4" x 9" rectangle into six 2 7/8" squares and cut each 2 7/8" square once diagonally. Each square will produce twelve half square triangles 2 7/8".

1. Photocopy or trace the number of triangle foundation papers necessary for your chosen quilt. The paper used will be three squares long x two squares wide.

Copy	Lap	24
	Double	40
	Queen	40

2. Place a 6 1/4" x 9" rectangle of background fabric right sides together with an 6 1/4" x 9" rectangle of leaf tip fabric. Construct half square triangles following the triangle foundation paper method detailed on page 15. Each rectangle pair will yield twelve half square triangle units measuring 2 1/2".

3. Repeat with all **B** and **D** rectangles.

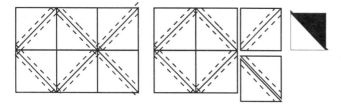

Leaf Stem Assembly

1. Center a leaf stem strip **G**, on the bias edge of a background half square triangle **C**. If need be, fold and finger crease to mark the center point of each piece. Stitch with a 1/4" seam and press the seam toward the leaf stem. The leaf stem strip will be oversized, and extend beyond the end of the triangle.

2. Center the sewn unit from step 1 on the bias edge of a second triangle **C**. Stitch and press the seam toward the leaf stem.

3. Trim the leaf stem square using the trimming **Template C** provided. If desired, center a 3/4" wide strip of masking tape along the bias line of a 4" square ruler, this may be used to trim the leaf stem unit.

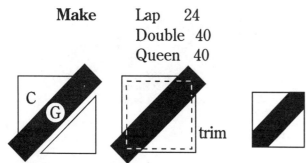

Make	Lap	24
	Double	40
	Queen	40

Leaf Block Assembly

1. For each leaf block, stitch pairs of three half square triangle units together as shown. Press the seams toward the leaf tips as indicated by the arrows. One strip will also receive a background square **A**, press this seam toward **A**.

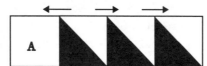

2. Stitch a leaf body rectangle **E** to one side of each leaf stem unit as shown. Press the seam toward **E**.

3. Stitch the matching leaf body rectangle **F** to a second side of the leaf stem unit as diagramed. Press this seam toward the leaf body rectangle **F**.

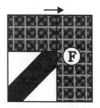

4. Stitch the shorter half square triangle strip to the unit from step 3 as diagramed below. Press the seam toward the leaf body.

5. Apply the second, longer, half square triangle strip. Press the seam toward the leaf body. The complete leaf block should measure 8 1/2" square.

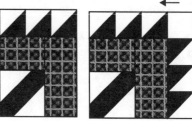

6. To simplify the construction of the quilt top, stitch the leaf blocks together in groups of 4 as diagramed.

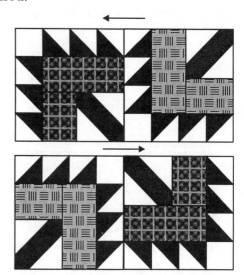

Tumbling Triangles Border

2" Half Square Triangle Units

NOTE The fabrics have been cut to allow for the use of triangle foundation papers when constructing half square triangles. If you wish to piece the triangles in the traditional method (triangle to triangle), cut each 6 1/4" square into four 2 7/8" squares and cut each 2 7/8" square once diagonally. Each square will produce eight half square triangles 2 7/8".

1. Photocopy or trace the number of triangle foundation papers necessary for your chosen quilt. The paper used will be two squares long x two squares wide.

Copy   Queen   38

2. Place a 6 1/4" square of background fabric right sides together with a 6 1/4" square of colored fabric. Construct half square triangles following the triangle foundation paper method detailed on page 15. Each square pair will yield eight half square triangle units measuring 2 1/2".

 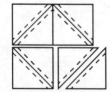

4" Half Square Triangle Units

1. Cut each 4 7/8" square in half once diagonally.

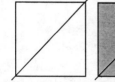

2. The 4" half square triangle units will be constructed by sewing two triangles together. Press the seam toward the colored fabric.

3. Cut each 5 1/4" square (one background and one dark fabric) twice diagonally, creating quarter square triangles.

4. Stitch each background quarter square triangle to a dark triangle. Press the seam toward the dark fabric.

5. Stitch the unit from step 4 to a 4 7/8" half square triangle from step 1. Press the seam toward the half square triangle.

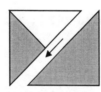 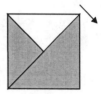

Border Construction

1. Stitch the 2 1/2" and the 4 1/2" triangle units together into the border components diagramed below.

 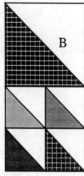

Make

Unit A   38
Unit B   38
Unit C   2
Unit D   2
Unit E   4

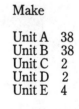

 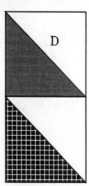 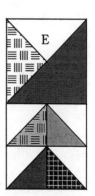

2. Join together the units listed to create two side borders.

     Join: 10 Unit A, 10 Unit B, and 1 Unit E

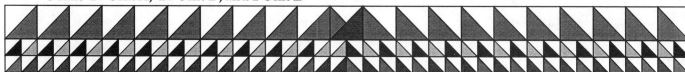

3. Join together the units listed to create the top and bottom borders.

     Join: 9 Unit A, 9 Unit B, 1 Unit C, 1 Unit D, and 1 Unit E.

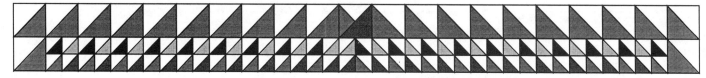

Quilt Top Assembly

1. Stitch the quilt top together into rows, and sew the rows together to form the quilt top: lap - 3 x 4, double - 4 x 5, and queen - 4 x 5.

2. Diagonally piece the first border, and cut lengths as needed. Attach side borders first and then the top and bottom border. Press all seams toward the border strips.

3. Queen Size Quilt: attach the pieced border units. Apply the side borders first, and then the top and bottom borders. Press the seams toward the first border.

4. Trim final borders to fit and apply to the quilt top, attach side borders first and then the top and bottom border strips. Press all seams toward the final border strips.

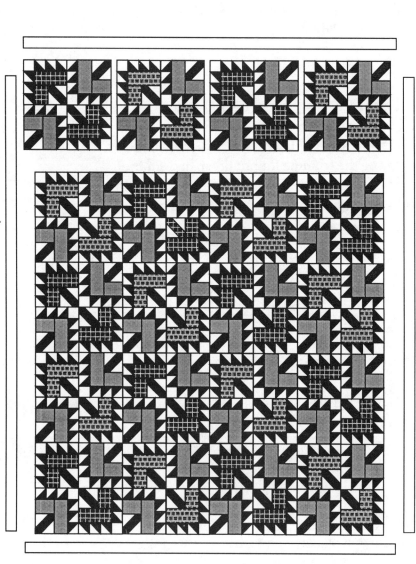

Autograph Lattice

Fabric Requirements

	Wall Hanging 41" x 51" 48 5" blocks	Lap 65" x 75" 120 5" blocks
Lattice - Light	3/4 yards	1 3/4 yards
Medium - Tan	3/4 yard	1 1/2 yards
Blue	1/2 yard	1 yard
Red	1/2 yard	1 yard
Purple	1/2 yard	1 yard
Green	1/2 yard	1 yard
First Border	1/2 yard	3/4 yard
Final Border	1 3/4 yards	2 1/4 yards
Binding	3/4 yard	3/4 yard
Backing	3 1/4 yards	4 3/4 yards

Cutting Instructions

	Wall Hanging	Lap
Lattice		
1 7/8" x 7 3/4" rectangle	48	120
Medium - Tan		
6 1/4" square	12	32
Blue		
6 1/4" square	3	8
2 1/2" x 3 1/4" rectangle	24	60
Red		
6 1/4" square	3	8
2 1/2" x 3 1/4" rectangle	24	60
Purple		
6 1/4" square	3	8
2 1/2" x 3 1/4" rectangle	24	60
Green		
6 1/4" square	3	8
2 1/2" x 3 1/4" rectangle	24	60
First Border		
2" strips	6	7
Final Border - sides	2 - 4 1/2" x 55"	4 - 6 1/2" x 79"
- top and bottom	2 - 4 1/2" x 52"	
Binding		
2 1/2" strips	6	8

1. Trim the 1 7/8" x 7 3/4" strips of lattice fabric as diagramed below, using **Template D**.

2. Layer the strips only as deep as you can accurately cut .

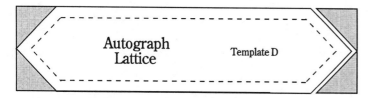

Autograph Lattice   Template D

Half Square Triangle Construction

NOTE The fabrics have been cut to allow for the use of triangle foundation papers when constructing half square triangles. If you wish to piece the triangles in the traditional method (triangle to triangle), cut each 6 1/4" square into four 2 7/8" squares and cut each 2 7/8" square once diagonally. Each square will produce eight half square triangles 2 7/8".

1. Photocopy or trace the number of triangle foundation papers necessary for your chosen quilt. The paper used will be two squares long x two squares wide.

Copy	Wall Hanging	12
	Lap	32

2. Place a 6 1/4" square of light fabric right sides together with a 6 1/4" square of dark fabric. Construct half square triangles following the triangle foundation paper method detailed on page 15. Each square pair will yield eight half square triangle units measuring 2 1/2".

3. If you are piecing the lap size quilt, each color family will produce a total of 64 half square triangle units. Only 60 units are required from each color family. Set aside four units from each group to use in another project. If you are sewing the wall hanging, do not set aside any units.

Grandmothers Choice Unit

This little trick was taught to me by Debbie Caffrey, of Debbie's Creative Moments.

Two half square triangle units are each sewn to a rectangle. The two resulting units are sewn together, and subcut - creating two identical Grandmother's Choice units. This greatly speeds piecing of this versatile unit.

1. Stitch each half square triangle unit to a 2 1/2" x 3 1/4" rectangle of the same color family: blue and blue, green and green, etc. Press the seam toward the rectangle.

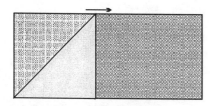

2. Stitch two units together. Match the raw edges. The seams **will not match.**

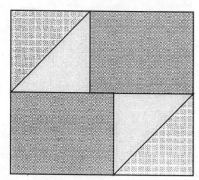

3. Carefully snip the seam allowance through the seam line at the center of the long seam. This will allow the seam allowance to be split and pressed in two different directions. Split the seam and press the seams toward the triangles. Place the pressed unit, right side up, on the cutting mat.

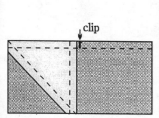
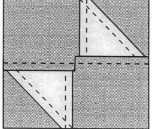

4. Align the **Omnigrid #96** ruler as diagramed below. Line up the 4" ruler marking with the left edge of the pieced unit. The 1 3/4" ruling will fall along the center seam, and the point of the ruler will extend past the fabric edge, allowing the "nub" line to align with the edge. Cut the pieced unit along the diagonal edge of the ruler, creating two identical grandmothers choice units. **Template E** has been provided if you do not have access to the **Omnigrid #96** ruler.

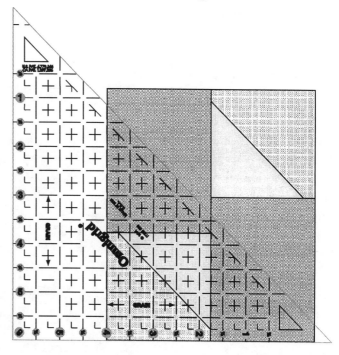

Block Construction

1. Gently finger press the lattice strip in half to lightly crease the center point. Match the center point of a grandmother's choice unit to the lattice strip, stitch, and press the seam toward the strip. Repeat with a second grandmother's choice unit.

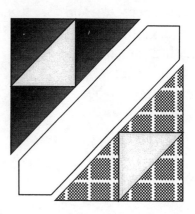

2. The blocks are assembled according to color. Follow the chart below to create the correct color combinations.

	Block ID	Wall Hanging	Lap
Purple/Red	A	12	30
Purple/Green	B	6	15
Purple/Blue	C	6	15
Red/Green	D	6	15
Red/Blue	E	6	15
Blue/Green	F	12	30

Quilt Top Assembly

1. Arrange the blocks on your floor or design wall, follow the diagram at the right to help you order the blocks in the proper color arrangement. Turn the blocks to group the grandmother's choice units with like colors.

2. Stitch the blocks into rows, and sew the rows together to form the quilt top: wall hanging - 6 x 8; and lap - 10 x 12.

3. Diagonally piece the first border strips together, cut lengths as needed, and apply to the quilt. Press the seams toward the border strip.

4. Trim final borders to fit and apply to the quilt top, attach side borders first, and then the top and bottom border strips. Press all seams toward the border strips.

All A Twinkle

Fabric Requirements

	Lap	**Queen**
	54" x 66"	90" x 102"
	20 12" blocks	56 12" blocks
Background - includes border	2 3/4 yards	6 yards
Solid Colors	1 3/4 yards	3 1/2 yards
Prints	1 3/4 yards	3 1/2 yards
Binding	5/8 yard	1 yard
Backing	3 1/2 yards	8 1/4 yards

Cutting Instructions

	1 Block	Lap	Queen
Background			
Final Border - cut first and set aside, lengthwise grain cut			
- sides		2 - 3 1/2" x 64"	2 - 3 1/2" x 100"
- top and bottom		2 - 3 1/2" x 58"	2 - 3 1/2" x 94"
3" square	4	80	224
4 3/8" square	4	80	224
Solid Colors			
2 1/8" x 21" strip	1	20	56
3 3/8" square	1	20	56
4 3/8" square	1	20	56
Prints			
2 1/8" x 21" strip	1	20	56
3 3/8" square	1	20	56
4 3/8" square	1	20	56
Binding			
2 1/2" strips		6	10

Block Construction

1. Stitch one solid 2 1/8" x 21" strip to its corresponding print strip using a 1/4" seam. Offset one end by 2" to allow for greater efficiency when subcutting the strip. Press the seam toward the solid fabric strip.

2. Align the **Omnigrid #98** ruler as diagramed below. Line up the 7" ruler marking with the bottom edge of the pieced strip. The tip of the ruler will fall off the edge of the sewn strip. Trim off the excess at the left of the ruler, and then cut along the right side of the ruler. Rotate the ruler and again cut along the right edge of the ruler. Each strip will yield 4 triangles. You may cut the strip using **Template F**, if the **Omnigrid #98** is not available in your area.

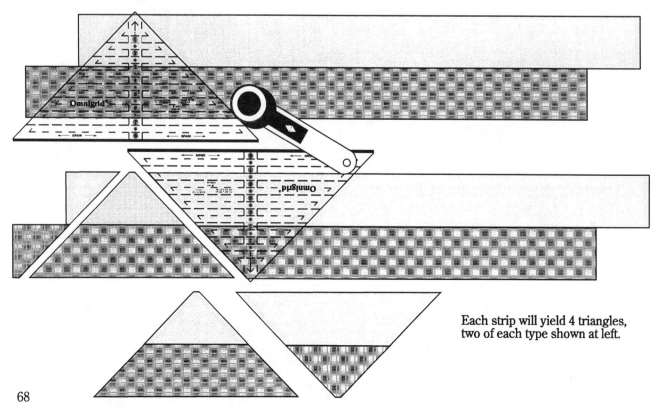

Each strip will yield 4 triangles, two of each type shown at left.

3. Cut each 3 3/8" and 4 3/8" square of solid and print fabric in half once diagonally.

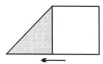 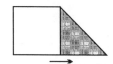

4. Stitch each 3 3/8" triangle to a 3" background square. Be sure to place the solid and print triangles as shown in relation to the square. Two solid and two print units will be needed for each block. Press the seam toward the triangle.

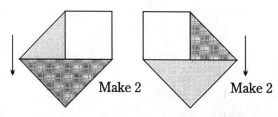

5. To each unit stitched in step #4, attach a 4 3/8" triangle. The print units will receive a 4 3/8" solid triangle, and the solid units will receive a 4 3/8" print triangle. Press the seam toward the 4 3/8" triangle.

Make 2   Make 2

6. Cut each 4 3/8" square of background fabric in half once diagonally. With pairs of triangles that are wrong sides together, trim each triangle pair into a kite shape. With the long edge of the triangle pair at the bottom, measure 4 3/8" from the point and cut. Triangles may also be trimmed using **Template G**.

Each triangle pair trimmed in this manner will yield mirror image kite pieces.

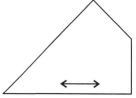 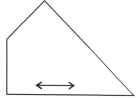

7. To each side of the unit from step #5 stitch a background kite. Be sure to place the fabric so that the bias edge will be sewn to the unit from step #5. This will place the straight grain along the outer edge of the block for greater stability. Press the seam away from the kite.

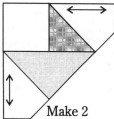 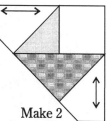

Make 2   Make 2

8. To each unit from step #7 attach a cut triangle unit. Be careful to place the solid fabric next to the print fabric as shown in the diagram. The seam will start and end at the 1/4" notch formed where the raw edges of the units meet. Press the seam toward the solid fabric.

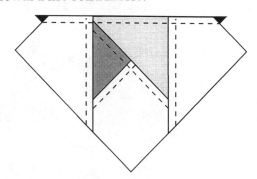

9. Make two of each unit for every block. The square should measure 6 1/2" raw edge to raw edge.

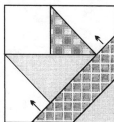 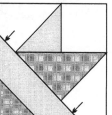

10. Stitch four squares together to form a block. Press the seams as diagramed. Each block should measure 12 1/2" measured from raw edge to raw edge.

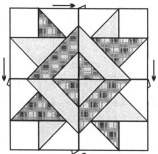

Quilt Top Assembly

1. Stitch the quilt top together into rows, and sew the rows together to form the quilt top: lap - 4 x 5, and queen - 7 x 8.

2. Trim final borders to fit and apply to the quilt top, attach the side borders first, and then the top and bottom borders. Press all seams toward the final border strips.

Whirligig

Fabric Requirements

	Lap	Double	Queen
	66" x 72"	80" x 96"	90" x 102"
	46 hexagons	86 hexagons	163 hexagons
Background	3 yards	4 1/2 yards	7 yards
Dark Fabrics	2 1/4 yards	3 1/2 yards	6 1/4 yards
Final Border	2 yards	2 3/4 yards	
Binding	3/4 yard	3/4 yard	1 yard
Backing	4 1/4 yards	6 yards	8 1/2 yards

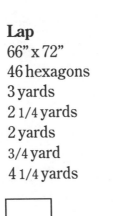

Cutting Instructions

Background	Lap	Double	Queen
Hexagon Piecing			
2 1/2" strips	25	43	83
Setting Triangles			
4 1/2" strips	3	4	6
First Border			
2 1/2" strips	6	8	
Dark Fabrics			
2 1/2" strips	25	43	83
Final Border - sides	2 - 6 1/2" x 60"	2 - 6 1/2" x 84"	
- top and bottom	2 - 6 1/2" x 70"	2 - 6 1/2" x 85"	
Binding			
2 1/2" strips	7 strips	9 strips	

Hexagon Construction

1. Stitch each dark strip to a background strip along the long edge. Offset one end by one inch to allow for greater efficiency when subcutting the 60 degree triangles. Press the seam toward the dark fabric strip.

2. To subcut your sewn strips, place the 4 3/4" marking of the **60 ° Clearview Triangle** ruler at the lower edge of your strip. The 2 1/2" ruler marking will be on the seam at the center of the sewn strip. The tip of the ruler will be off the edge of your fabric. Trim off the waste at the left edge of the ruler, and then cut along the right edge of the ruler. Rotate the ruler and again cut along the right edge of the ruler. You may cut the strip using **Template H**, if the ruler is not available in your area.

3. Each strip should yield seven dark triangles and seven light triangles.

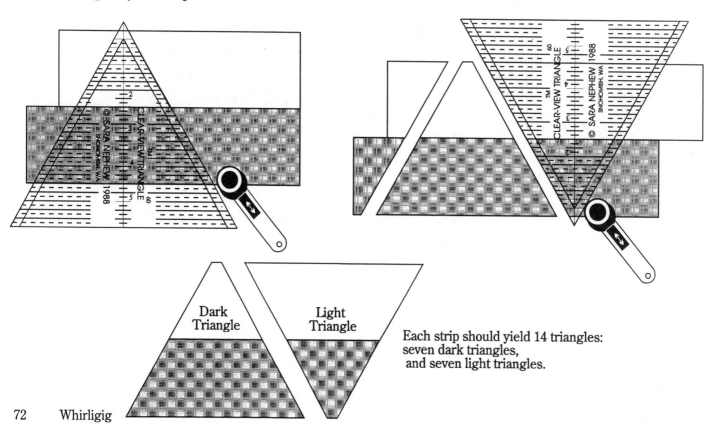

Each strip should yield 14 triangles: seven dark triangles, and seven light triangles.

4. Stitch two triangles together as diagramed below. Press the seam toward the dark fabric. Repeat with a second pair of triangles.

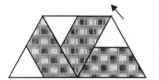 

Make 2 for each hexagon

5. Add the third triangle. Press the seam toward the dark fabric. This will give you two identical half hexagons. Leave these in half hexagon form. The quilt top will be assembled in rows of half hexagons.

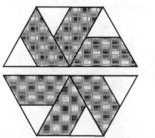

6. Repeat steps 4 and 5 using all dark triangles. Hexagons created using the dark triangles are labeled as Positive Hexagons.

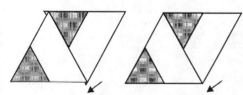

Positive Hexagon

7. Stitch two triangles together as diagramed below. This time using the light triangles. Press the seam toward the light triangle. Repeat with a second pair of triangles.

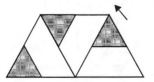 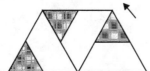

Make 2 for each hexagon

8. Add the third triangle. Press the seam toward the light fabric. This will give you two identical half hexagons. Leave these in half hexagon form.

9. Repeat steps 7 and 8 using all light triangles. Hexagons created using the light triangles are labeled as Negative Hexagons.

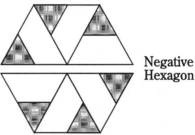

Negative Hexagon

Each strip combination will yield one positive hexagon and one negative hexagon. After stitching all of the half hexagons together, you will be left with a number of unmatched triangles. These may be sorted according to color and sewn into mismatched half hexagons which can also be used in the quilt. Be sure not to mix positives and negatives together in the same hexagon.

Setting Triangles

Place the 4 1/2" wide strips of background fabric on the cutting mat folded, **wrong sides together.** This will allow you to cut Template I and Template I reversed at one time. Cut the strips into the number of units listed below using **Template I** and **Template J**.

	Lap	Double	Queen
Template I	14	20	26
Template I-r	14	20	26
Template J	6	8	12

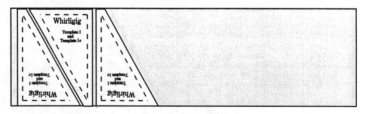

Folded strip of fabric used to produce Template I and I-r.

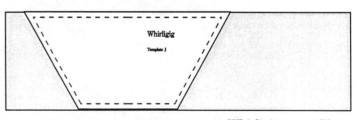

Quilt Top Assembly

1. Arrange the half hexagons on your floor or design wall.

2. Study the two quilts pictured in the quilt gallery. One quilt isolates the positive hexagons in the center of the quilt. The second model spreads the positive hexagons in a diagonal swish across the quilt. Rearrange the hexagons until you find an arrangement that pleases you. It may be helpful to use an instant camera to photograph your work in progress so that you do not lose your favorite arrangement in the shuffle.

3. Stitch the half hexagons together into rows. Beginning and ending each row with a Template I piece. Care must be taken as you are stitching rows together to match seams.

4. Diagonally piece the first border strips together, cut lengths as needed, and apply to the quilt. Press the seams toward the border strips. (The queen size quilt does not receive any borders.)

5. Trim final borders to fit and apply to the quilt top, attach side borders first, and then the top and bottom borders. Press all seams toward the border strips.

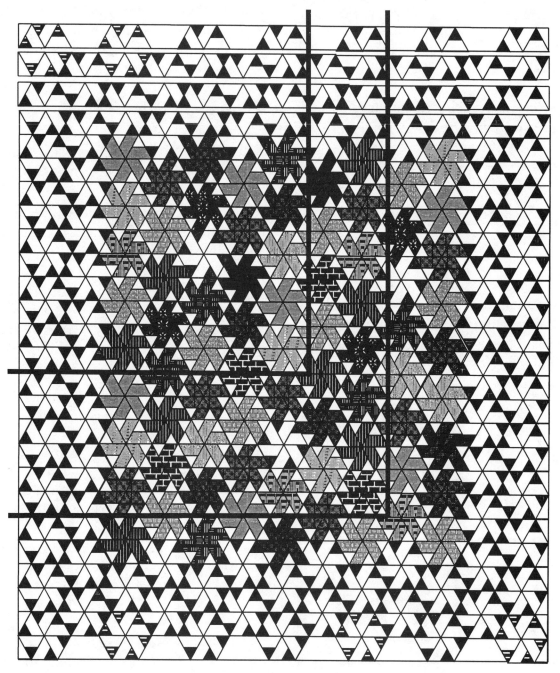

Kaleidoscope

Fabric Requirements

	Wall Hanging 72" square 81 6" blocks	**Twin** 72" x 96" 117 6" blocks	**Queen** 96" x 108" 195 6" blocks
Light Fabrics	2 1/2 yards	3 yards	5 yards
Medium Fabrics	1 1/2 yards	1 3/4 yards	2 3/4 yards
Dark Fabrics	2 1/2 yards	3 1/4 yards	5 yards
Final Border	2 1/4 yards	2 3/4 yards	3 yards
Binding	3/4 yard	3/4 yard	1 yard
Backing	4 1/2 yards	6 yards	8 3/4 yards

Cutting Instructions

Light Fabrics	Wall Hanging	Twin	Queen
3 1/2" strips	10	14	23
2 5/8" strips	13	18	28
Medium Fabrics			
3 1/2" strips	10	14	23
Dark Fabrics			
3 1/2" strips	21	29	46
Final Border - sides	2 - 6 1/2" x 64"	2 - 6 1/2" x 88"	2 - 6 1/2" x 100"
- top and bottom	2 - 6 1/2" x 76"	2 - 6 1/2" x 76"	2 - 6 1/2" x 100"
Binding			
2 1/2" strips	8	10	11

Strip Subcutting

1. To subcut the strips, place the 6" block line of the **Kaleido-Ruler** at the lower raw edge of your 3 1/2" strip. Trim off the waste at the left edge of the ruler, and then cut along the right edge of the ruler. Rotate the ruler and again cut along the right edge. You may cut the strip using **Template K** if the **Kaleido-ruler** is not available in your area. Each strip should yield 20 triangles. Refer to the chart at the right for the appropriate number of triangles.

2. Place a folded 3 1/2" strip on the cutting mat. Cut the strip using **Template L**. Cutting this template from a folded strip, creates **Template L** and **Template L-r** at the same time. Refer to the chart for the number of triangles to cut.

	Wall	Twin	Queen
Light			
Template K	200	280	448
Medium			
Template K	200	280	448
Dark			
Template K	360	512	836
Template L	40	48	60
Template L-r	40	48	60

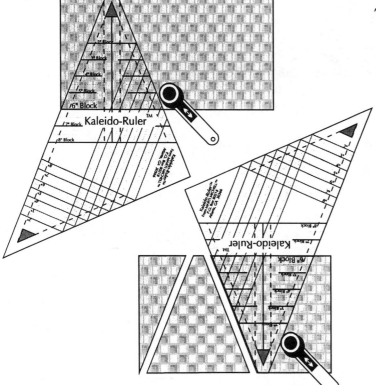

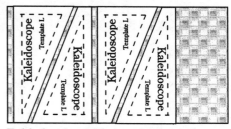

Folded strip of fabric used to produce Template L and Template L-r.

Block Legend

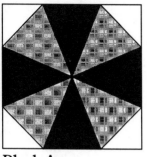 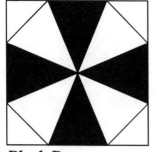 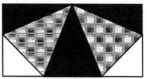 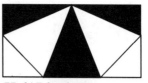

Block A Block B Half Block A Half Block B Corner

Finished Block Size: 6" x 6"

	Wall Hanging	Twin	Queen
Block A	41	59	98
Block B	40	58	97
Half Block A	16	20	26
Half Block B	20	24	30
Corner Block	4	4	4

3. Cut the 2 5/8" strips of light fabric into 2 5/8" squares. Cut each square once diagonally to create half square triangles.

Cut	Wall Hanging	200 squares » 400 triangles
	Twin	280 squares » 560 triangles
	Queen	448 squares » 896 triangles

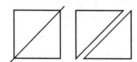

Block Assembly

1. Stitch a dark triangle **K** to a light (or medium) triangle **K,** always placing the dark **K** on top. Stitch from the wide end to the point. Press the seam toward light (medium) triangle.

2. Stitch two pairs together. Sew from the wide end to the point. The light (medium) triangle will be on top this time. Align the raw edges and tightly butt the opposing seams to guarantee that all points will match. Press the seam toward the dark fabric.

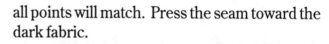
 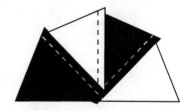

3. Stitch two block halves together. The seams on each will be opposing. Pin the seam intersection for the best results.

4. After checking that the points match, pull the two or three stitches of the vertical seam that extend past the long seam into the 1/4" seam allowance. This will allow the final seam to be swirled and pressed so that all of the seams are rotating in one direction, distributing the bulk in the center of the block.

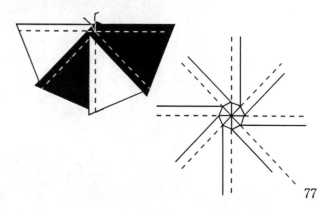

5. Stitch a 2 5/8" half square triangle of light fabric to each light (or medium) triangle **K**. This seam should begin and end at the 1/4" notch where the raw edges intersect. Press the seams toward the half square triangle. Repeat to make the number of complete blocks necessary for your chosen quilt as listed at the top of page 77.

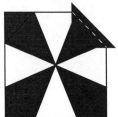 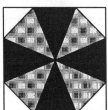 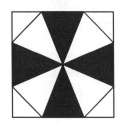

6. Assemble half blocks, using piece **L** and **L-r** of dark fabric at the top edge of the unit. Press the seams in one direction. Attach two 2 5/8" half square triangles to complete the half blocks.

7. Assemble the corner squares.

Quilt Top Assembly

1. Stitch the quilt top together into rows, and sew the rows together to form the quilt top: wall hanging - 9 x 9; twin - 9 x 13; and queen - 13 x 15. It is a good idea to match pin seam intersections for the best results.

2. The half blocks can be added to the beginning and ending of each row, or they may be joined together as independent units and applied in the manner of a border as diagramed below.

3. Trim final border strips to fit and apply to the quilt top, attach the side borders first, and then the top and bottom border strips. Press the seams toward the border strips.

Chapter 6 Finishing

Borders

All of the quilts in this book were constructed using square borders. The application of a square border is easier to master than the application of a mitered border.

Primary Borders

Primary borders are all border strips that are attached to the quilt top before the final border. They may be very narrow, wide, piped, or even pieced. All primary borders for the quilts in this text were cut as crossgrain strips and pieced together using diagonal seaming. Diagonal seams in the border strips are less visible than straight seams, no effort is made to place the seams in any particular position.

To make a diagonal seam, place the first strip right side up. Position the second fabric strip right side down, on top of the first strip. The second strip will be placed at a right angle to the first. Stitch diagonally across the strip ends. Trim the excess to 1/4" and press the seam to one side. All of the "First (Second or Third) Border" strips are sewn together to create a long strip, and the necessary lengths are cut from it.

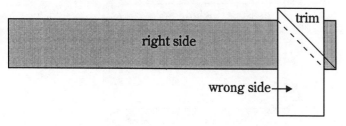

Pieced Borders

A pieced border is a wonderful addition to a beautiful quilt. A pieced border must be mathematically correct to fit the quilt top. If your piecing has been less that accurate, it is possible to adjust the vertical seams of the border strip to accommodate the difference. Unfortunately, this will also adjust where the points of the pieced border fall.

Piped Border

Piped borders are especially fun in places that you would like a little "hit" of color. The piped border strips are pieced diagonally to create a long strip. Trim the excess fabric to 1/4" seam allowance and press these seams open. Press the 1" wide strip in half lengthwise - wrong sides together. This will result in a 1/2" wide strip.

The piped border strips are cut to length and basted to the edge of the quilt top, raw edges even. The strips will remain in this position, with the fold toward the center of the quilt. After the next border is applied, the piped border will measure 1/4" wide.

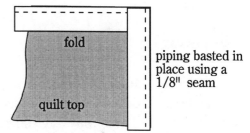

Final Border

The final border is cut from the lengthwise grain of the fabric. This will require extra yardage to be purchased, but it is well worth the expense.

The lengthwise grain of the fabric is more stable than the crossgrain. This extra stability will go a long way toward preventing stretching and ruffling of the quilt edge due to handling.

To cut a lengthwise fabric strip, measure the inches of fabric called for in the directions, and cut the yardage to that length. Fold the fabric crosswise, until it is narrow enough to be spanned by your rotary ruler. The folded fabric will have selvage at either edge. The first cut will be to remove the selvage. Cut the border strips to size. Use the rulings on the cutting mat if your ruler is too narrow.

Applying Borders

The individual quilt instructions in this text do not give exact measurements for the borders. The strip measurements given are longer than what would be mathematically correct. No matter how carefully you have pieced, over the course of **many** seams, variations do occur. It is not uncommon for the sides of a quilt top to have stretched with the handling that they have received, or even measure differently. These variations need to be addressed if you wish to have a square quilt that lays flat.

To accommodate the variations, do not cut a strip to the length that is mathematically correct, and do not stitch a long length to the side of the quilt top and cut it off where the edge of the quilt lands!!

Measuring

When adding borders it is important to measure the "body" of the quilt top, not the edges of the quilt that may have stretched.

1. Press the quilt top carefully. When measuring, it is important that the quilt lay as flat and smooth as possible.

2. Measure from top to bottom through the center of the quilt with a metal measuring tape. My sewing bag contains a petite 10 foot tape measure. Cut the two side borders to that measurement.

3. Pin the border strips in place along the sides of the quilt top. Match the center of the border strip to the center of the quilt top. Use as many pins as necessary.

4. Stitch the border strip to the quilt top. You are making the quilt top fit the border strip! Stitch with the border strip on top. The feed dogs will help to ease in the fullness of the quilt top if necessary.

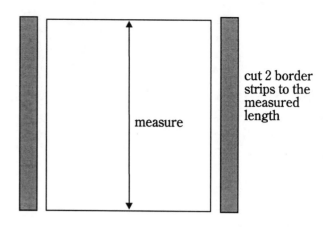

cut 2 border strips to the measured length

measure

5. From the right side, press the seams toward the border strips.

6. Lay the quilt on a flat surface and measure the quilt top from side to side through the center of the quilt, including the border pieces that you just added. Cut the top and bottom border strips to that measurement.

7. Pin and stitch these borders in the same manner that the side borders were added.

8. Press the seams toward the border strip.

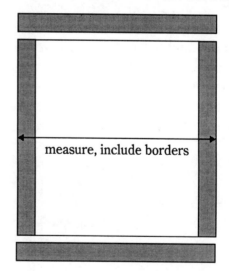

measure, include borders

All borders will be added in this manner. When applying the final border, backtack the seams that will be exposed at the raw edge of the quilt. This helps to prevent the stitches from pulling out as the quilt top is layered and quilted. The quilts in this book have had the side borders applied first, and then the top and bottom borders. This order of border application is generally a more economical use of fabric - a shorter yardage of fabric is required.

Backing

How to prepare the backing is a matter of personal taste. Many quilters use the leftover scraps of the quilt top to piece together a scrappy backing. If you are planning to hand quilt the layers, a pieced backing may not be the best idea. The many seams might be difficult to "needle". Fortunately, fabric manufacturers are thinking about backings, and have made available fabric that is 100" - 112" wide. This fabric is very easy to use; simply cut to size. There are no seams to make the quilting process difficult.

Select a backing fabric that is a good quality cotton. Do not purchase a poor quality piece of fabric because it is less expensive. The backing needs to wear as well as the quilt top. A bed sheet really is not an ideal quilt backing. The fabric of a bed sheet is very tightly woven, and may make hand quilting a chore, perhaps even a painful experience.

The effect of the backing fabric color needs to be considered. If a polyester batting is used, a dark backing fabric may show through, dulling the light or bright colors of the quilt top. If the backing is patterned, the quilt top may appear splotchy! Cotton batting is more opaque and will permit less shadowing.

Yardage Requirements

Backing should be 6" - 8" larger than the completed quilt top. Yardage is figured on 43" of usable fabric width after preshrinking and removing the selvages. Measure the quilt top to determine the length and width.

- widths up to 37"   length   + 6"

- widths 38" to 80"   (length x 2) + 12"
   Remove the selvages and sew one
   lengthwise seam. Press to one side.

- widths greater than 80"   (width x 3) + 18"
   Remove the selvages and sew two
   crosswise seams. Press to one side
Press the seam open if you plan to hand quilt.

Batting

Batting is the layer of filling between the quilt top and the backing. There are many weights and types of batting available on the market today. It is available in polyester, cotton, cotton/polyester blends and even wool. Batting is available packaged in standard sizes or as yardage from a bolt. Some are better suited to hand quilting while others are best left for tying.

Bonded Polyester

Polyester has been widely used as batting for many years. It has been in just the last few years that cotton and cotton /polyester blends have started to reclaim the market. Polyester batts are available in different weights and thicknesses. The thinner polyester batts mimic the look of a cotton batt, and are easy to hand quilt. The thicker batts are difficult to hand quilt and are used for hand tied quilts.

Polyester fibers tend to migrate. Once the fibers reach the surface of the quilt top, they ball together. This migration is called bearding. Polyester batting is especially guilty of this problem and it is particularly visible on dark quilts. A grey polyester batting is available for use in dark quilts, making the bearding less noticeable.

100% Cotton or Cotton/Polyester Blends

The cotton battings will give a more traditional look to your quilts. 100% cotton batting generally requires more quilting than a polyester batting would, but batting manufacturers are constantly upgrading and improving their product. The traditional cotton batting needs to be quilted every 1/4" - 1/2" to prevent the fibers from clumping. Cotton batting is available today that can be quilted 8" apart!

Hobbs Heirloom Cotton batting is my personal favorite. I prefer the antique look that the Hobbs batting gives. Cotton/ polyester batting hand quilts nicely and is a great choice for machine quilting. As you select and purchase batting, my best advice is to read the package!! Know what you are working with to prevent disappointment.

Quilting

Quilting is the process by which the three layers of the quilt (top, batting and backing) are held together. Quilting can be accomplished by hand or by machine. And, if you have no inclination to quilt, the three layers can be held together by tying.

Entire books are available on the subject of quilting, both hand and machine. I will refer you to your local quilt shop. They can help you find the text that you need.

Binding

Binding is the process of finishing the edge of the quilt after it is quilted.

Preparation
• Baste the edge of the quilt top down. This can be done with a long, wide zig-zag stitch on the sewing machine. This basting will prevent excess shifting of the quilt top layer at the edge as the binding is applied.
• Trim the batting and backing 1/8" beyond the raw edge of the quilt top. This extra fabric and batting will fill out the binding and prevent empty spaces.
• Piece the cut binding strips together using a diagonal seam. Trim the seams to 1/4" and press the seams open.
• Press the long binding strip in half lengthwise, right side out, to a width of 1 1/4".

Attach the Binding
• Position the binding strips so that its lengthwise raw edges are even with the raw edge of the quilt top. Start stitching 1/4" from the corner of the quilt top, backtack to secure the seam and stitch to the opposite end. Stop stitching 1/4" from the quilt corner and backtack.
• Remove the quilt from the sewing machine, and snip threads. Rotate the quilt to prepare to sew the next edge.
• Fold the binding strip up, away from the quilt, it will fold nicely at a 45° angle. Fold it again to

bring the strip edge along the raw edge of the quilt top, leaving a 2"- 3" tail of binding extending beyond the corner. Lower the needle into the binding at the point where the first seam stopped, 1/4" from the corner of the quilt top, backtack and stitch to the opposite corner of the quilt top.
• Continue around the quilt in this manner until you reach the corner where you began stitching. Fold the first section binding strip out of the way as you stitch to the end of the final binding length. Stitch to 1/4" from the corner and backtack.

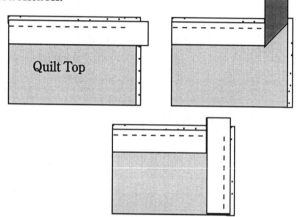

Mitered Corners
• To finish the corners of the binding, fold the tail of the binding so that it lays flat. Draw a line perpendicular to the seam line, starting at the end of the seam, **A**. Draw a second line at a 45° from the first line, **B**. Draw a third line, **C**, at a 45° from the opposite end of line **A**. The intersection of lines **B** and **C** will be a 90° angle.

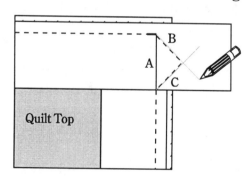

• With a small stitch, sew directly on lines **B** and **C**, pivot at the point, and backtack at each end of the seam. Trim to a 1/4" seam allowance. Turn the stitched corner right side out.
• Roll the binding over the raw edge of the quilt. Hand stitch the fold of the binding to the stitching line on the backside of the quilt.

Triangle Foundation Paper Masters

Quilt Size	Copies

Foundation A - 1" Half Squares

- **Fabric cut 4 1/4" x 4 1/4".**
- Each unit will yield 8 half square triangle units.

Cabin Fever Bears

	Quilt Size	Copies
	Wall Hanging	5
	Queen	16

Foundation B - 2" Half Squares

- **Fabric cut 6 1/4" x 6 1/4".**
- Each unit will yield 8 half square triangle units.

Tablescraps - border

	Quilt Size	Copies
	Wall Hanging	11
	Twin	12
	Queen	16

Road To Oklahoma

	Lap	24
	Double	40
	Queen	60

Corn and Beans

	Twin	36
	Queen	63

Cabin Fever Bears

	Wall Hanging	8
	Queen	40

Falling Leaves

	Queen Border	38

Autograph Lattice

	Wall Hanging	12
	Lap	32

- **Fabric cut 6 1/4" x 9".**
- Each unit will yield 12 half square triangle units.

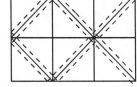

Falling Leaves

	Lap	24
	Double	40
	Queen	40

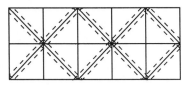

- **Fabric cut 6 1/4" x 15".**
- Each unit will yield 12 half square triangle units.

Tablescraps

	Quilt Size	Copies
	Wall Hanging	16
	Twin	24
	Queen	48

Foundation C - 3" Half Squares

- **Fabric cut 8 1/4" x 8 1/4".**
- Each unit will yield 8 half square triangle units.

Friendship Star

	Lap	35
	Twin	56
	King	110

Foundation A - 1" Half Squares
1 1/2" when measured from raw edge to raw edge

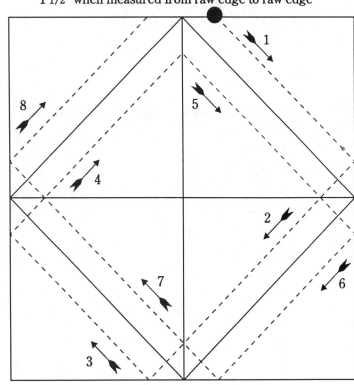

Foundation B - 2" Half Squares
2 1/2" when measured from raw edge to raw edge

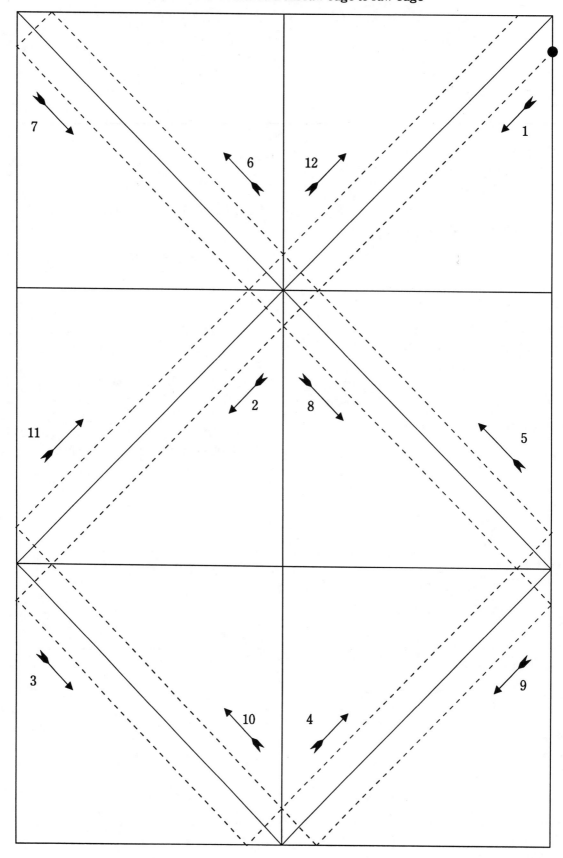

Foundation C - 3" Half Squares

3 1/2" when measured from raw edge to raw edge

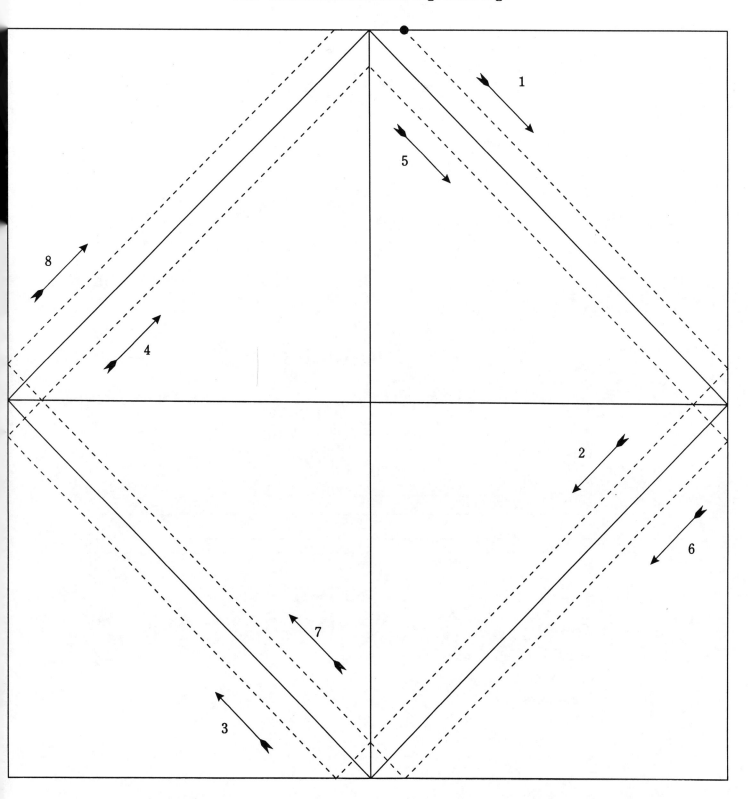

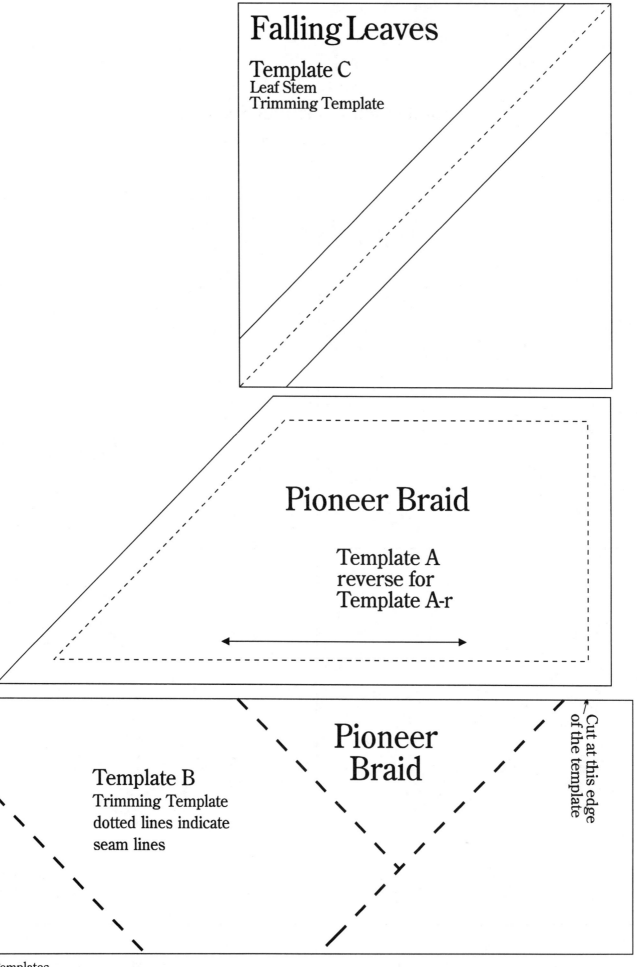

Falling Leaves

Template C
Leaf Stem
Trimming Template

Pioneer Braid

Template A
reverse for
Template A-r

Pioneer Braid

Template B
Trimming Template
dotted lines indicate
seam lines

Cut at this edge
of the template

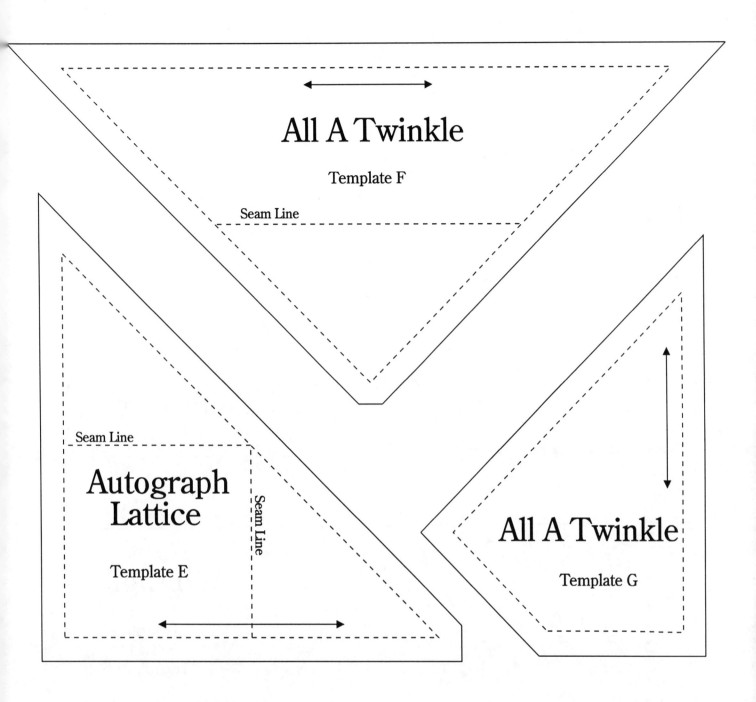

All A Twinkle

Template F

Seam Line

Seam Line

**Autograph
Lattice**

Template E

Seam Line

All A Twinkle

Template G

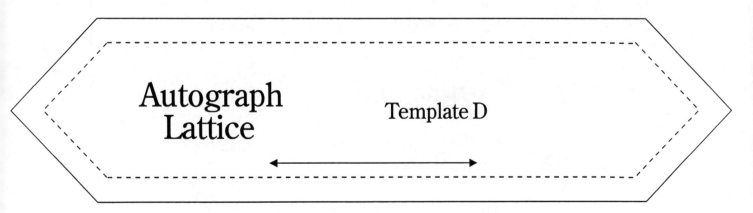

**Autograph
Lattice**

Template D

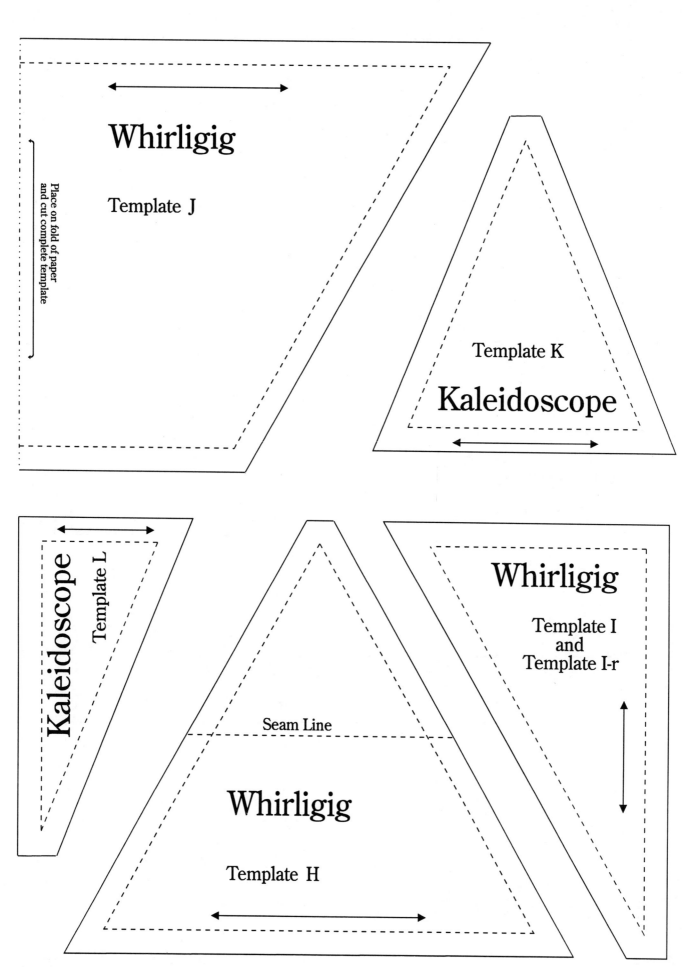

Whirligig

Template J

Place on fold of paper and cut complete template

Template K

Kaleidoscope

Kaleidoscope

Template L

Whirligig

Template I
and
Template I-r

Seam Line

Whirligig

Template H

Quilter's Cheat Sheet

Half Square Triangles

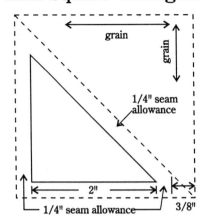

Finished Size + 7/8" = Cut Square

Quarter Square Triangles

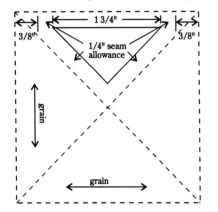

Finished Size + 1 1/4" = Cut Square

Corner Triangles

A diagonal set quilt requires a half square triangle at each corner to complete the quilt top.

A = the known block measurement
B = the unknown measurement

$A \div 1.414 = B$
$B + 7/8" =$ Cut size of square
Each square will yield 2 triangles.

Setting Triangles

A diagonal set quilt requires quarter square triangles to fill in the gaps along the sides of the quilt top.

A = the known block measurement
B = the unknown measurement

$A \times 1.414 = B$
$B + 1 1/4" =$ Cut size of square
Cut square will yield four triangles.

Bias Binding

Bias binding is a must for quilts with curved edges, and a longer wearing treatment for bed quilts. Crossgrain binding has a single thread that runs the length of the outermost edge of the quilt. A worn spot can easily open up the length of the quilt. With a bias binding, the threads run across the edge diagonally. One weak thread can cause only local damage. Yardage requirements are the same for crossgrain bindings and bias bindings.

Cut a single layer of yardage at a 45° angle. Stitch selvages together using a 1" wide seam. Trim selvages to 1/4" and press the seam open. Cut yardage into bias strips 2 1/2" wide. Stitch the strip ends together. Press the seams open. Fold bias strip in half, wrong side together. Bind the quilt in the usual fashion.

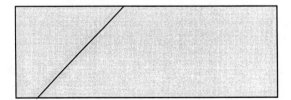

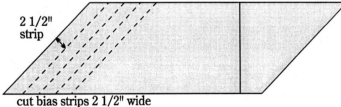

2 1/2" strip

cut bias strips 2 1/2" wide

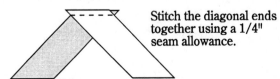

Stitch the diagonal ends together using a 1/4" seam allowance.

Standard Sizes

	Mattress	Batting	Quilt
Crib	23" x 46"	45" x 60"	37" x 52" - 56"
Twin	39" x 75"	72" x 90"	70" x 90" - 96"
Double	54" x 75"	81" x 96"	80" x 90" - 96"
Queen	60" x 80"	90" x 108"	90" x 96" - 100"
King	76" x 80"	120" x 120"	104" x 96" - 100"

Mattress size + desired drop = quilt size. *Drop* is the portion of the quilt that falls below the edge of the mattress. Consider the usage of the quilt when determining the drop.

Backing Yardages

Backing should be 6" to 8" larger than the completed quilt top. Yardage is figured on 43" of usable fabric width after shrinkage and selvage elimination. Measure the quilt top to determine the length and the width.

Single Length
Widths up to 37" = length + 6"

Two Lengths
Widths 38" to 80" = (length x 2) + 12"
Remove the selvages and sew one lengthwise seam. Press to one side.

Three Widths
Widths greater than 80" = (width x 3) + 18"
Remove the selvages and sew two crosswise seams. Press to one side.

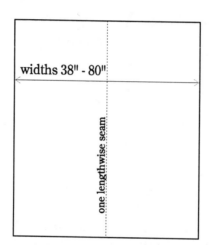

Quilt Top / width up to 37" | widths 38" - 80" / one lengthwise seam | widths greater than 80" / crosswise seam / crosswise seam

Mitered Binding

Stitch binding to the quilt edge. Start and stop the seam 1/4" from the quilt corner. Backtack at each end. Fold the strip away from the quilt top, and then down into position to stitch the second edge. Start and stop the seam 1/4" from the quilt corners. Continue in this manner around the quilt.

Draw lines **A**, **B**, and **C** as shown. Stitch on lines **B** and **C**. Trim excess and turn point right side out. Hand stitch fold in place.

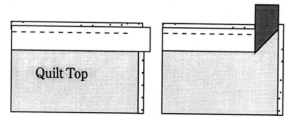

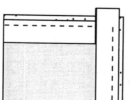

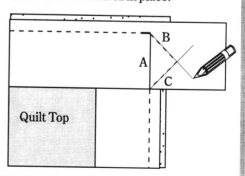

Meet the Author

Brenda Henning is a compulsive quiltmaker with a fondness for traditional design and a desire to incorporate todays speed piecing techniques with yesterdays well-loved patterns. Brenda's machine sewing experience began at the early age of 10 on her grandmother's treadle sewing machine with the first quilt following at age 14. Brenda became a compulsive quilter in the mid-'80s, and began teaching quiltmaking in 1989, after her third child turned one.

Writing and self-publishing that work have been by-products of teaching quilting. Brenda is the author of: *Alaskan Silhouette Sampler* and *Sampler Schoolhouse*, along with numerous individual patterns available under the label *Bear Paw Productions*.

Brenda lives in Anchorage, Alaska, with her husband, Richard, and their three children, Beth, Christi and Joshua. Two Rottweilers, Coco and Blue (I'll bet you can't guess Brenda's favorite color!) share copious quantities of black dog hair with every quilt that leaves the premises.

Brenda is a member of the Valley Quilters Guild in Palmer, Alaska, and teaches regularly at The Quilt Tree and Quilt Works in Anchorage as well as for other shops and guilds throughout Alaska.

Other Books and Patterns by Brenda Henning

Books

Alaskan Silhouette Sampler
Sampler Schoolhouse

Patterns

- Chugach Pines
- Cat Nap
- Mountain Paintbrush
- New York Beauty
- Celtic Love Knot
- Dawn of the North
- Flannel Star
- Scrap Hunter

Stained Glass Patterns

- Hummingbird
- Wild Roses
- Wild Poppies
- Wild Iris
- Forget-Me-Not
- Crescent Santa
- Elf

These books and patterns are available at your local quilt shop or from:

Bear Paw Productions
4015 Iona Circle
Anchorage, AK 99507
(907) 349-7873

Sources

Specialty products used in the text are listed below. Please check with your local quilt shop for availability of the product before you contact the manufacturer directly. Support your local shop!

Omnigrid #96 and **Omnigrid #98 rulers**
Omnigrid, Inc.
1560 Port Drive
Burlington, WA 98233

Kaleido-Ruler™
Michell Marketing, Inc.
3525 Broad Street
Chamblee, GA 30341
(770) 458-6500

60° Clear-View Triangle Ruler
Clearview Triangle
8311 - 180th Street S.E.
Snohomish, WA 98296-4802
(360) 668-4151

TRIANGLES ON A ROLL
Gridded Half Square Triangle Paper
Dutton Designs
P.O. Box 7646
Chandler, AZ 85246-7646
(602) 940-9682

Triangle Paper™
SPPS, Inc./Quiltime
4410 N. Rancho Dr., #165
Las Vegas, NV 89130
(702) 658-7988

Hobbs Bonded Fibers
200 S. Commerce Dr.
Waco, TX 76710